OHIO STATE

DAILY DEVOTIONS FOR DIE-HARD FANS

BUCKEYES

OHIO STATE

Daily Devotions for Die-Hard Fans: Ohio State Buckeyes
© 2012 Ed McMinn
Extra Point Publishers; P.O. Box 871; Perry, GA 31069

Library of Congress Cataloging-in-Publication Data
13 ISBN Digit ISBN: 978-0-9846377-6-8

Manufactured in the United States of America.

Unless otherwise noted, scripture quotations are taken from the *Holy Bible, New International Version*. Copyright © 1973, 1978, 1984, by the International Bible Society. All rights reserved.

Visit us at www.die-hardfans.com.

Cover and interior design by Slynn McMinn.

Every effort has been made to identify copyright holders. Any omissions are unintentional. Extra Point Publishers should be notified in writing immediately for full acknowledgement in future editions.

BUCKEYES

You can go become a tiger, a bear, a lion, or any other animal that is a mascot at schools across this country, but there is only one place in this world you can become a Buckeye.

-- Woody Hayes

The following titles are available:

Alabama Crimson Tide
Arkansas Razorbacks
Auburn Tigers
Clemson Tigers
Duke Blue Devils
Florida Gators
Florida State Seminoles
Georgia Bulldogs
Georgia Tech Yellow Jackets
Kentucky Wildcats
LSU Tigers
Michigan Wolverines
Mississippi Rebels
Mississippi State Bulldogs
North Carolina Tar Heels
NC State Wolfpack
Ohio State Buckeyes
Oklahoma Sooners
Penn State Nittany Lions
South Carolina Gamecocks
Tennessee Volunteers
Texas Longhorns
Texas A&M Aggies
Virginia Cavaliers
Virginia Tech Hokies
and NASCAR

IN THE BEGINNING

Read Genesis 1, 2:1-3.

"God saw all that he had made, and it was very good" (v. 1:31).

A student wrote off for a rule book, and the coach rode a pony to practice. Such was the beginning of football at Ohio State.

As early as 1887, students at the university got hold of one of those newfangled "foot-balls" and started playing around with it. The balls were rare, though, as only those few students with extra cash in their pockets could afford one. Sometimes, the boys made a ball out of whatever they could find. On other occasions, several boys took up collections to get a real store-bought ball.

George Cole, class of 1891, assumed a leadership role in getting football off to an official and organized start. He wrote Spalding's for a rule book and also talked former classmate Alexander S. Lilley, who had attended Princeton, into coaching the football team without pay. Lilley, who lived several miles from campus, rode a pony to practice. Former Princeton All-American K.L. Ames also helped out, teaching the would-be players how to kick the ball.

On May 3, 1890, Ohio State University played its first college football game, against Ohio Wesleyan at Delaware. It was not exactly the complex and sometimes dazzling game we see today. There was no passing, and the emphasis was on power plays. As Cole put it, "Anything went except brass knuckles. . . . It was all right to step on a man's face as long as care was exercised in the performance."

The local newspapers ignored one of the most historic days in school history. Only the student newspaper, *The Lantern*, reported on the game, which started at 9:30 a.m.

State led 14-6 at the half, but Wesleyan tied the game with ten minutes to play. *The Lantern* reported that Ohio State "formed a flying wedge and scored on the second attempt from four feet out." That touchdown made the final score 20-14.

Fittingly, Ohio State football had begun with a win.

Beginnings are important, but what we make of them is even more important. Consider, for example, how far The Ohio State University football program has come since that first season. Every morning, you get a gift from God: a new beginning.

God hands to you as an expression of divine love a new day full of promise and the chance to right the wrongs in your life. You can use the day to pay a debt, start a new relationship, replace a burned-out light bulb, tell your family you love them, chase a dream, solve a nagging problem . . . or not.

God simply provides the gift. How you use it is up to you. People often talk wistfully about starting over or making a new beginning. God gives you the chance with the dawning of every new day. You have the chance today to make things right – and that includes your relationship with God.

It is safe to say that foot ball [sic] has taken a firm hold upon both the students and citizens.
                    -- Delaware Gazette *on the first-ever OSU football game*

**Every day is not just a dawn;
it is a precious chance to start over or begin anew.**

DAY 2

JUST AN ILLUSION

Read Habakkuk 1:2-11.

"Why do you make me look at injustice? Why do you tolerate wrong? Destruction and violence are before me; there is strife, and conflict abounds" (v. 3).

Tears started to fill quarterback Craig Krenzel's eyes. "I couldn't believe we had lost," said cornerback Dustin Fox. As it turned out, though, the defeat was just an illusion.

The Buckeyes were solid underdogs when they met the Miami Hurricanes -- winners of 34 straight -- in the 2003 Fiesta Bowl for the national championship. They played the game of their lives in forcing the game into overtime, but when a fourth-down pass fell incomplete after Miami had scored on its possession, the season was apparently over. The Canes celebrated; fireworks lit up the Arizona sky. The Buckeyes were stunned and devastated.

But things were not what they seemed. One referee hesitated because he wanted to get the call right. When he was convinced, he threw a flag: pass interference in the end zone. "I fell to my knees," said sophomore running back Lydell Ross. "Then I heard the announcer say, 'Wait a minute. There's a flag on the field.'"

After security officials cleared the field, Krenzel scored on third down and Mike Nugent kicked the PAT to send the game into a second overtime. Freshman running back Maurice Clarett scored from five yards out on the fifth play to propel the Buckeyes into a 31-24 lead.

Desperate to save themselves, the Canes faced fourth and goal form the 2. "I'm bringing the juice," said linebacker Cie Grant when he saw the formation. He brought it, wrapping up Miami's quarterback and forcing a heave to nowhere and nobody.

The Buckeye defeat had been an illusion after all. On the other hand, victory and the national title were real.

Sometimes in football -- like the loss to Miami -- things just aren't what they seem. It's the same way in life: what seems to be reality sometimes isn't at all.

In our violent and convulsive times, we must confront the possibility of a new reality: that we are helpless in the face of anarchy; that injustice, destruction, and violence are pandemic in and symptomatic of our modern age. Anarchy seems to be winning, and the system of standards, values, and institutions we have cherished appears to be crumbling while we watch.

But we should not be deceived or disheartened. God is in fact the arch-enemy of chaos, the creator of order and goodness and the architect of all of history. God is in control. We often misinterpret history as the record of mankind's accomplishments -- which it isn't -- rather than the unfolding of God's plan -- which it is. That plan has a clearly defined end: God will make everything right. In that day things will be what they seem; God's ultimate triumph will be real.

Nothing is ever as good as it seems or as bad as it seems.
-- Former Clemson coach Curley Hallman

The forces of good and decency often seem
helpless before evil's power, but don't be fooled:
God is in control and will set things right.

DAY 3

THOSE THINGS

Read Matthew 5:43-48.

*"He causes his sun to rise on the evil and the good, and
sends rain on the righteous and the unrighteous" (v. 45).*

Those things -- bad breaks in the form of sudden and unexpected injuries -- are an unfortunate part of any athlete's life. For Andrew Armstrong, though, the bad break was worst than most, what he called "a death sentence" to his career.

Armstrong came to Ohio State in 2007 with plans of being a star starting pitcher. He had a promising freshman season, going 4-3 with the third-best ERA on the team. During a winter practice, though, he noticed pain in his left shoulder when he threw. "I was like man, this isn't normal," he recalled. "This was just something different, like a whole new ballgame of pain."

It was. The pain stayed for his sophomore season, which was rocky. He had a 2-3 record and an 11.51 ERA.

During the summer, an orthopedic surgeon diagnosed the problem: a torn labrum, a piece of cartilage that holds the shoulder together. Even with surgery, recovery was uncertain. Therapists warned him his rehab would be the worst six months of his life.

For Armstrong, being away from the game was more difficult than the agony of his therapy. "I got lost from baseball," he said of the 2010 season, for which he received a medical redshirt. "I cared about the team and the guys, but I didn't matter to the team."

"I had to learn how to throw again," he said. With a lot of help from assistant coach Mike Stafford, he did just that. He returned for the 2011 season, though not as a starter. The coaches were not willing to have him throw that many pitches that hard.

Armstrong had a solid year. He led the league with 33 appearances, all in relief. He went 2-0 with a 3.68 ERA. Senior outfielder Brian DeLucia appreciated what Armstrong had done. "A lot of guys don't bounce back from that injury," he said.

Like Andrew Armstrong, you've probably had a few of "those things" in your own life: bad breaks that occur without regard to justice, morality, or fair play. You wonder if everything in life is random with events determined by a roll of some cosmic dice. Is there really somebody scripting all this with logic and purpose?

Yes, there is; God is the author of everything.

We know how it all began; we even know how it all will end. It's in God's book. The part we play in God's kingdom, though, is in the middle, and that part is still being revealed. The simple truth is that God's ways are different from ours. After all he's God and we are not. That's why we don't know what's coming our way, and why "those things" catch us by surprise and dismay us when they do occur.

What God asks of us is that we trust him. As the one – and the only one – in charge, he knows everything will be all right for those who follow Jesus.

It's like a death sentence to pitchers.
-- Andrew Armstrong on the torn labrum he suffered

Life confounds us because, while we know the end and the beginning of God's great story, we are part of the middle, which God is still writing.

DAY 4

IN A WORD

Read Matthew 12:33-37.

*"For out of the overflow of the heart the mouth speaks.
The good man brings good things out of the good stored
up in him, and the evil man brings evil things out of the
evil stored up in him" (vv. 34b-35).*

Rarely does a head football coach manage to annoy both the opponent and his own team's fans with his post-game comments, but Woody Hayes did just that following the 1955 Rose Bowl.

The undefeated Buckeyes won the Football Writers' Association's national championship on Jan. 2 by whipping Southern Cal 20-7. Ohio State finished behind UCLA in the wire service polls, but since the Bruins had played in the Rose Bowl the year before, they were ineligible for a return trip. That ranking rankled the Buckeye coaching legend, who was quite vocal in his contention that Ohio State had played a tougher schedule than had UCLA.

The 1955 contest was unusual in that for the first time in the bowl game's storied history, it rained. Early in the second quarter, senior Buckeye quarterback Dave Leggett, the game's MVP, scored from the three to cap a 69-yard drive. Following the kickoff, he recovered a Trojan fumble and then threw a 21-yard touchdown pass to senior running back Bobby Watkins, the team's leading scorer that season. In only one minute and 20 seconds, Ohio State had scored enough points to win the game.

After the game, Hayes riled up the West Coast sportswriters by

BUCKEYES

asserting that at least five teams in the Big Ten could have beaten Southern Cal. He provided equal opportunity insults, however, when he criticized the bands for being on the wet field at halftime. Hayes said the musicians had chopped up the field too much for either team to play well in the second half. The coach's candid remark wasn't taken too kindly back home since the school had gone to great expense and trouble to get the 120-piece marching band to Pasadena.

Even more so than in Woody Hayes' time, everybody's got something to say these days and likely as not a place to say it. Talk radio, 24-hour sports and news TV channels, late-night talk shows, post-game interviews. Talk has really become cheap.

But words still have power, and that includes not just those of the talking heads, hucksters, and pundits on television, but ours also. Our words are perhaps the most powerful force we possess for good or for bad. The words we speak today can belittle, wound, humiliate, and destroy. They can also inspire, heal, protect, and create. Our words both shape and define us. They also reveal to the world the depth of our faith.

We should never make the mistake of underestimating the power of the spoken word. After all, speaking the Word was the only means Jesus had to get his message across – and look what he managed to do.

We must always watch what we say, because others sure will.

Don't talk too much or too soon.

-- Bear Bryant

Choose your words carefully; they are the most powerful force you have for good or for bad.

DAY 5

BE PREPARED

Read Matthew 10:5-23.

*"I am sending you out like sheep among wolves. Therefore
be as shrewd as snakes and as innocent as doves" (v. 16).*

Why are we working on all this new and different stuff if we never run it in the games?" Buckeye players asked that question frequently early in Jim Tressel's tenure. The answer was simple: He was preparing them for Michigan.

Writer Jeff Snook once said Tressel prepared for Michigan the whole year. His players learned quickly how much truth there was to that statement. In his first season (2001), Tressel had his team work on some plays and formations in August that weren't used at all in September or in October. Running back Maurice Hall (2001-04) expressed the players' bewilderment: "We had no idea why we were doing it," he said.

They found out why when they played Michigan. For the first time, Tressel used an unbalanced-line formation his team had prepared. It caught Michigan off guard, and Jonathan Wells ran for three touchdowns in the first half. OSU won 26-20.

In 2002, the Buckeyes trailed 9-7 late in the game and ran an option to the right side. Hall scored the game-winning TD -- on a play they had practiced but had not run all season.

In the monumental clash of 2006, the Buckeyes used a play they had set Michigan up for with their play-calling in previous games. Tressel moved wide receiver Ted Ginn, Jr., to tight end and called for a bomb to him on second and inches. In every second and short situation during the previous month, State had run tailback Chris Wells straight ahead. This time, quarterback Troy Smith faked to Wells and straightened up and passed to Ginn for a 39-yard touchdown.

Even in August, Tressel was preparing his team for Michigan.

You know the importance of preparation in your own life. You went to the bank for a car loan, facts and figures in hand. That presentation you made at work was seamless because you practiced. The kids' school play suffered no meltdowns because they rehearsed. Knowing what you need to do and doing what you must to succeed isn't luck; it's preparation.

Jesus understood this, and he prepared his followers by lecturing them and by sending them on field trips. Two thousand years later, the life of faith requires similar training and study. You prepare so you'll be ready when that unsaved neighbor standing beside you at your backyard grill asks about Jesus. You prepare so you will know how God wants you to live. You prepare so you are certain in what you believe when the secular, godless world challenges it.

And one day you'll see God face to face. You certainly want to be prepared for that.

None of the players ever question anything we are working on because we know it may be used in the biggest game of the season.
-- Maurice Hall on plays OSU practiced but didn't run in games

**Living in faith requires constant study
and training, preparation for the day
when you meet God face to face.**

WHAT A SURPRISE!

Read 1 Thessalonians 5:1-11.

"But you, brothers, are not in darkness so that this day should surprise you like a thief" (v. 4).

I'm already writing my concession speech," admitted Woody Hayes. Then his Buckeyes and he got quite a surprise.

The 1973 showdown with Michigan was one for the ages. Both teams were unbeaten, and the Buckeyes were ranked No. 1. They had a big problem, though: soph quarterback Cornelius Greene's thumb was swollen twice its normal size. "I have a plan," Hayes told his concerned assistants.

The plan was simple: Greene was taken out of the game, doing little except handing the ball off to Archie Griffin and fullback Pete Johnson. Greene didn't attempt a single pass until the final minute when the Buckeyes desperately tried to break a 10-10 tie.

The deadlock left both teams with 7-0-1 records in the conference, but UM was 10-0-1 compared to OSU's 9-0-1. The Big Ten athletic directors would vote to decide who would go to the Rose Bowl. The outcome seemed a foregone conclusion.

In the locker room after the game, UM head coach Bo Schembechler was upbeat and optimistic. He said he believed his team, which had outgained OSU in the game, deserved the berth in the Rose Bowl. Hayes, on the other hand, remained quiet when asked if his team deserved the bid. "I have no opinion on the Rose Bowl," he said. "If we're selected, we'll go."

BUCKEYES

Back home in Ann Arbor, Schembechler remained confident while a despondent Hayes quietly prepared his team for a let-down. One reason Hayes was so sure Michigan would get the vote was his realization of his unpopularity within the conference.

But then came the surprise. By a vote of 6-4, the ADs selected Ohio State. Schembechler went ballastic, tearing up furniture at a press conference; Hayes just smiled and called his wife.

Surprise birthday parties are a delight. And what's the fun of opening Christmas presents when we already know what's in them? Some surprises in life provide us with experiences that are both joyful and delightful (such as an unexpected Rose Bowl).

Generally, though, we expend energy and resources to avoid most surprises and the impact they may have upon our lives. We may be surprised by the exact timing of a baby's arrival, but we nevertheless have the bags packed beforehand and the nursery all set for its occupant. Paul used this very image (v. 3) to describe the Day of the Lord, when Jesus will return to claim his own and establish his kingdom. We may be caught by surprise, but we must still be ready.

The consequences of being caught unprepared by a baby's insistence on being born are serious indeed. They pale, however, beside the eternal effects of not being ready when Jesus returns. We prepare ourselves just as Paul told us to (v. 8): We live in faith, hope, and love, ever on the alert for that great, promised day.

I just went nuts.
-- Linebacker Randy Gradishar on learning of the Rose-Bowl vote

**The timing of Jesus' return will be a surprise;
the consequences should not be.**

DAY 7

UNEXPECTEDLY

Read Matthew 24:36-51.

"No one knows about that day or hour, not even the angels in heaven, nor the Son, but only the Father" (v. 36).

Terrelle Pryor may have been the MVP of the 2011 Sugar Bowl, but he didn't pull off the most unexpected play of the game, the one that sealed the Buckeyes' win over Arkansas.

As the Jan. 4 game approached, Pryor and four of his teammates "maneuvered [themselves] squarely into the crosshairs of the NCAA SWAT team by admitting to having signed and sold team memorabilia." Thus, the junior quarterback was under additional pressure not to let everyone down in the Sugar Bowl.

He didn't. He threw for 221 yards and two touchdowns and ran for 115 yards in leading the 6th-ranked Buckeyes (12-1) to a 31-26 win over 8th-ranked Arkansas (10-3).

Thanks to an unusual touchdown, the Buckeyes took a quick lead. They marched 74 yards in eight plays, the score coming on a 37-yard Pryor run. Only he didn't get into the end zone. He dropped the ball at the 3, and senior wide receiver Dane Sanzenbacher -- who was voted the team's MVP for the season -- rounded up the loose piece of leather in the end zone for the touchdown.

The Buckeyes didn't slow down in the first half, taking a 28-10 lead into the locker room at the break. But Arkansas mounted a furious last-half rally, and it took that unexpected play from an unexpected player to nail down the win in the last minute.

BUCKEYES

Arkansas closed to within five at 31-26 and -- to the horror of Buckeye fans everywhere -- blocked a punt with just over a minute left. The Razorbacks were 18 yards away from a touchdown.

But along came reserve lineman Solomon Thomas to save the day. He drifted into coverage and intercepted the first pass of his collegiate career with 58 seconds left. Unexpectedly, the drama was over as Pryor took a knee and ran out the clock.

Just as Arkansas did in the Sugar Bowl, we think we've got everything figured out and under control, and then something unexpected (like Solomon Thomas) happens. About the only thing we can expect from life with any certainty is the unexpected.

God is that way too, suddenly showing up to remind us he's still around. A friend who calls and tells you he's praying for you, a hug from your child or grandchild, a lone lily that blooms in your yard -- unexpected moments when the divine comes crashing into our lives with such clarity that it takes our breath away and brings tears to our eyes.

But why shouldn't God do the unexpected? The only factor limiting what God can do in our lives is the paucity of our own faith. We should expect the unexpected from God, this same deity who caught everyone by surprise by unexpectedly coming to live among us as a man, and who will return when we least expect it.

[My quarterback] did exactly what he was coached to do. When they blitzed, they clicked out a lineman he didn't see.
— Arkansas coach Bobby Petrino on the unexpected interception

God continually does the unexpected,
like showing up as Jesus,
who will return unexpectedly.

DAY 8

THE GREATEST

Read Mark 9:33-37.

"If anyone wants to be first, he must be the very last, and the servant of all" (v. 35).

While The Ohio State University has showcased many great athletes over the decades, only one can rightfully claim to be "the world's greatest athlete of his era." That would be Jesse Owens.

"No individual's accomplishments cast a larger shadow than those of Jesse Owens," wrote former newspaper sports editor Dan McGrath for the Big Ten Network. He was speaking, of course, of Owens and the 1936 Olympics.

Even before that, though, Owens had become a national star as the "Buckeye Bullet." On May 25, 1935, he pulled off what has forever been known as the "seminal moment" for college track and field. At the Big Ten meet, he set three world records and tied a fourth within 45 minutes. His performance to this day is regarded as "the greatest individual accomplishment in track and field history." During that storied junior season at Ohio State, Owens competed in forty-two events and won them all. While in Columbus, Owens won eight NCAA championships, four each in 1935 and in 1936.

In 1936, though, Owens' national fame was eclipsed by his worldwide acclaim and stature as a result of the Olympics in Berlin. With the world not far away from war, Adolf Hitler used the games as a pulpit for Nazi propaganda and a showcase for so-

called "Aryan racial superiority."

On the world's biggest sports stage, Owens both surprised and annoyed Hitler and his cronies by winning four gold medals: the 100-meter dash, the 200-meter dash, the long jump, and the 4x100-meter relay. That performance has been called "a landmark event in the history of Ohio State, the big Ten Conference, the United States, the Olympic Games and of the 20th century."

It just doesn't get any greater than that.

We all want to be the greatest. The goal for the Buckeyes and their fans every season is the national championship. The competition at work is to be the most productive sales person on the staff or the Teacher of the Year. In other words, we define being the greatest in terms of the struggle for personal success. It's nothing new; Jesus' disciples saw greatness in the same way.

As Jesus illustrated, though, greatness in the Kingdom of God has nothing to do with the secular world's understanding of success. Rather, the greatest are those who channel their ambition toward the furtherance of Christ's kingdom through love and service, rather than their own advancement. This, of course, is a complete reversal of status and values as the world sees them.

After all, who could be greater than the person who has Jesus for a brother and God for a father? And that's every one of us.

[Jesse Owens] won four gold medals [in the Olympics], a performance that established [him] as the world's greatest athlete beyond question.
-- Former Chicago Tribune *sports editor Dan McGrath*

To be great for God has nothing to do with
personal advancement and everything to do with
the advancement of Christ's kingdom.

DAY 9

A SECOND CHANCE

Read John 7:53-8:11.

"'Then neither do I condemn you,' Jesus declared. 'Go now and leave your life of sin'" (v. 8:11).

Football teams often get a second chance to win a game; occasionally, they may even get a third chance. But a fourth chance? Ohio State did once.

Wes Fesler is one of the greatest athletes in Ohio State history, a nine-letter winner with three each in football, baseball, and basketball, a three-time All-American end/fullback, and an All-Big Ten selection in basketball. He was named the head football coach after the 1946 season.

The Buckeyes struggled through a 2-6-1 campaign in Fesler's first year, but the Northwestern game that season provided one of the most memorable finishes in Ohio State gridiron history.

The Buckeyes trailed 6-0 when they were stopped at the Wildcat 1-yard line with 1:47 left in the game. They forced Northwestern to punt and took over at the Cat 36 with only 31 seconds left. Quarterback Pandel Savic led a desperation drive that moved to the Northwestern 12 with 13 seconds to play.

But time ran out as the Cats intercepted a pass. Quite a few fans left Ohio Stadium believing Northwestern had won. "I remember I had already pulled out my hip pads thinking the game was over," recalled OSU running back Joe Whisler. But Northwestern had twelve men on the field on the play, and State got another play from the 7.

Given a second chance, Fesler called for a run, but halfback Rodney Swinehart was stopped at the 2. Again, the game appeared to be over. This time, though, Northwestern was offside. State got one more play. On the team's third chance, Savic hit end Jimmy Clark for the game-tying touchdown. The PAT was blocked, however, apparently ending the game in a tie.

Incredibly, Northwestern was again offside. Given a fourth chance to win the game, the Buckeyes pulled it out when Emil Moldea's second kick was good.

"If I just had a second chance, I know I could make it work out." Ever said that? If only you could go back and tell your dad one last time you love him, take that job you passed up rather than relocate, or replace those angry shouts at your son with gentle encouragement. If only you had a second chance, a mulligan.

As the story of Jesus' encounter with the adulterous woman illustrates, with God you always get a second chance. No matter how many mistakes you make, God will never give up on you. Nothing you can do puts you beyond God's saving power. You always have a second chance because with God your future is not determined by your past or who you used to be. It is determined by your relationship with God through Jesus Christ.

God is ready and willing to give you a second chance – or a third chance or a fourth chance – if you will give him a chance.

I was on the field for [the game-winning PAT] without the hip pads.
-- Joe Whisler

You get a second chance with God
if you give him a chance.

DAY 10

COMEBACK KIDS

Read Luke 23:26-43.

"Jesus answered him, 'I tell you the truth, today you will be with me in paradise'" (v. 43).

The Buckeyes once pulled off what was at the time the biggest comeback in college football history.

"Anything that could go wrong went wrong," said quarterback Greg Frey about the first half of the Minnesota game of Oct. 28, 1989. Head coach John Cooper said of the first thirty minutes, "That was probably the worst half I've ever been associated with."

Four Buckeye turnovers led to 24 Minnesota points, and with five minutes left in the first half, the Gophers led 31-0. Ohio State scored one second before halftime when tailback Carlos Snow scored on fourth down. Frey passed to junior wide receiver Jeff Graham for the conversion to make it 31-8.

Still, few were honestly thinking of winning the game. "I told them to get out there and fight for their lives," Cooper said of his halftime talk. "Sometimes you have to accept the fact that it is not our day, just get out of there and go home," Frey said about his thoughts when the score ran to 31-0. Still, "I made myself focus on getting back in the game."

The Buckeyes did more than that. Frey threw for 327 yards and three touchdowns in the second half to lead college football's greatest comeback ever to that time. OSU started the second half with a drive that netted a field goal. Then came touchdown passes

to Snow and Graham, a Frey TD on an option, and the game-winner, a 15-yard toss to Graham with 51 seconds left. Ohio State put 23 points on the board in the last quarter to win 41-37.

"To this day, " Frey said years later, "people come up to me and tell me where they were when they saw that game." After the game, Minnesota's fans and Frey shared the same sentiment, which he expressed by saying, "I still can't believe it."

"I've never been more proud of a football team," Cooper said about his comeback kids.

Life will have its setbacks whether they result from personal failures or from forces and people beyond your control. Being a Christian and a faithful follower of Jesus Christ doesn't insulate you from getting into deep trouble. Maybe financial problems suffocated you. A serious illness put you on the sidelines. Or your family was hit with a great tragedy.

Life is a series of victories and defeats. Winning isn't about avoiding defeat; it's about getting back up to compete again. It's about making a comeback of your own.

When you avail yourself of God's grace and God's power, your comeback is always greater than your setback. You are never too far behind, and it's never too late in life's game for Jesus to lead you to victory, to turn trouble into triumph. As it was with the Buckeyes of '89 and the thief on the cross who repented, it's not how you start that counts; it's how you finish.

I didn't think there was any way possible they could come back.
-- Minnesota defensive end Eddie Miles on the '89 game

In life, victory is truly a matter of how you finish
and whether you finish with Jesus at your side.

DAY 11

GOOD NEWS

Read Matthew 28:1-10.

'"He has risen from the dead and is going ahead of you into Galilee. There you will see him.' Now I have told you" (v. 7).

Brian Baschnagel didn't get the news he had been drafted by the Chicago Bears directly. He eventually got it sort of third-hand -- thanks to his mischievous roommate.

A running back, Baschnagel had the misfortune to be in the 1972 recruiting class with a fellow Buckeye named Archie Griffin. After his first game of '72, he started thinking about transferring. Later in the season, though, the starting wingback, Rich Galbos, was injured, and Baschnagel was moved into the spot. "I guess it was a blessing in disguise," he said. He became a much more rounded player. "I learned to block, and they threw me passes," he said. "Once in a while they threw me a bone and I ran a counter."

He was a team captain as a senior in 1975 for the 11-1 Big-Ten champions. The day of the NFL draft in April 1976 was a busy one for him. A two-time Academic All-America, Baschnagel had an 8 a.m. class, a test, and a paper to turn in. With all that, he forgot about the draft until he was walking back to his apartment.

His roommate was quarterback Garry McCutcheon. The two friends started a rousing game of gin when Baschnagel returned. As they played, McCutcheon nonchalantly said, "By the way, the Steelers called and wanted to know if you would like to play for

BUCKEYES

them. I told them I thought you would." They played a few more hands before McCutcheon spoke up again. "The Redskins also called. . . . I told them that you would [play for them]."

More hands passed before McCutcheon said, "By the way, congratulations. You were drafted by the Chicago Bears in the third round." Thus did Baschnagel receive some of the biggest news of his life. He had a nine-year pro career with the Bears.

The story of mankind's "progress" through the millennia could be summarized and illustrated quite well in an account of how we disseminate our news. For much of recorded history, we told our stories through word of mouth, which required time to spread across political and geographical boundaries. That method also didn't do much to ensure accuracy.

Today, though, our news – unlike Brian Baschnagel's -- is instantaneous. Yesterday's news is old news; we want to see it and hear about it as it happens.

But the biggest news story in the history of the world goes virtually unnoticed every day by the so-called mainstream media. It is, in fact, often treated as nothing more than superstition. But it's true, and it is the greatest, most wonderful news of all.

What headline should be blaring from every news source in the world? Certainly this one: "Jesus Rises from Dead, Defeats Death." It's still today's news, and it's still the most important news story ever.

I could have killed him.
-- Brian Baschnagel on the way his roommate told him news of the draft

**The biggest news story in history took place
when Jesus Christ walked out of that tomb.**

DAY 12

A DOG'S LIFE

Read Genesis 6:11-22; 8:1-4.

*"God remembered Noah and all the wild animals and the
livestock that were with him in the ark" (v. 8:1).*

Around Cassie Dickerson's house, disdain for Michigan runs
so deep even the family dog is a part of it.

Dickerson is the first All-America in the history of the Ohio
State women's soccer program, earning the honor following the
2010 season. She was also the Big Ten Defensive Player of the
Year. The two-year starter at center back was a major reason the
2010 team went 17-5-2, won the program's first Big-Ten title, and
advanced to the semifinals of the NCAA championships.

When Cassie was growing up, her mother taught ballet at Western Michigan University. She had thoughts of her daughter taking
after her, so she enrolled her in a class -- which didn't last very
long. "I was also taking Tae Kwon Do at the time," the younger
Dickerson explained. "My mother got tired of me karate chopping
and kicking the other girls in the class." So -- to Cassie's embarrassment -- the mother did some kicking of her own, booting her
daughter out of the class. Cassie did stay with the Tae Kwon Do,
though, ultimately earning a black belt.

When the time came for Dickerson to make a decision about
college, only one thing was certain: "There was no way [she] was
headed to Ann Arbor." Her father grew up in Elyria, Ohio, and
played football at Western Michigan. He carefully groomed his

BUCKEYES

family to be Buckeye fans. "I never looked at Michigan," Dickerson said. "My dad said he would never pay a cent to Michigan."

That grooming of the family to be Buckeye fans included Rico, the family Rottweiler.

As Dickerson explained it, Rico "sits to 'Buckeye,' lays down to 'touchdown' and plays dead when we say 'Wolverine.'"

Do you have a dog or two like Rico around the place? How about a cat that passes a lot of her time staring longingly at your caged canary? Kids have gerbils? Maybe you've gone more exotic with a tarantula or a ferret.

We Americans do love our pets; in fact, more households in this country have pets than have children. We not only share our living space with animals we love and protect but also with some – such as roaches and rats – that we seek to exterminate.

None of us, though, has ever faced anything remotely like what Noah did when he packed God's menagerie into one boat. God expressly determined the dimensions of the ark to accommodate his creatures. He thus saved all his varmints from extinction, including the fish, the frogs, and the ducks, who must have been quite delighted with the whole flood business.

The lesson is clear for we who strive to live as God would have us: All living things are under God's care. God doesn't call us to care for and respect just our beloved pets; we are to serve God as stewards of all of his creatures.

It's not the size of the dog in the fight but the size of the fight in the dog.
-- Archie Griffin

God cares about all his creatures,
and he expects us to respect them too.

DAY 13

PROMISES, PROMISES

Read 2 Corinthians 1:16-20.

"No matter how many promises God has made, they are 'Yes' in Christ" (v. 20).

Dimitrious Stanley made a pair of promises. He kept them and thus was a crucial part of a big Buckeye win.

The 1997 Rose Bowl looked like trouble for OSU. The '96 squad had won its first ten games to clinch the Big Ten title, but Michigan pulled off the upset, costing the Buckeyes a shot at the national title. Instead, Pac-10 champ Arizona State was the bunch talking about a championship with Ohio State as the stepping stone.

The Sun Devils led 10-7 early in the third quarter when Stanley fulfilled the promises he had made. A senior wide receiver who led the team in catches that season, Stanley noticed early on that ASU's defense was designed to give the wideouts the middle of the field. Repeatedly in the first half, he told the coaches and his quarterback that they should throw him the ball over the middle. "I promise I'll score," he said. At halftime, Stanley cornered quarterbacks coach Walt Harris and made the same promise to him.

Somebody finally listened. On the second play following the Arizona State field goal, quarterback Joe Germaine hit Stanley over the middle. As he had promised, Stanley scored, completing a 72-yard play, the longest pass reception in Buckeye bowl history.

The touchdown also fulfilled another promise he had made. The day before the game during the team's walk-through, Stanley had stood in the end zone that said 'Ohio State,' pointed to a spot, and told senior lineman Matt Finkes, "I'm going to score right here tomorrow." "That very spot is where I scored," Stanley said.

The Buckeyes took a thrilling 20-17 win when Germaine hit freshman David Boston with a touchdown pass from the ASU 5 with only 19 seconds to play.

For Dimitrious Stanley, the game meant promises made and promises kept.

The promises you make don't say much about you, but the promises you keep tell everything. The promise to your daughter to be there for her softball game. To your son to help him with his math homework. To your parents to come see them soon. To your spouse to remain faithful until death parts you. And remember what you promised God?

You may carelessly throw promises around, but you can never outpromise God, who is downright profligate with his promises. For instance, he has promised to love you always, to forgive you no matter what you do, and to prepare a place for you with him in Heaven.

And there's more good news in that God operates on this simple premise: Promises made are promises kept. You can rely absolutely on God's promises. The people to whom you make them should be able to rely just as surely on your promises.

In the everyday pressures of life, I have learned that God's promises are true.

-- Former major leaguer Garret Anderson

**God keeps his promises just as those
who rely on you expect you to keep yours.**

DAY 14

YOU DECIDE

Read John 6:60-69.

"The words I have spoken to you are spirit and they are life. Yet there are some of you who do not believe" (vv. 63b-64a).

Ohio State's faculty council once made an unexpected decision that under today's bowl setup would be impossible. It cost the Buckeyes a shot at the national title.

Woody Hayes' football teams won consensus national championships in 1954, 1957, and 1968. Each of those seasons was capped off by a win in the Rose Bowl. The 1961 Buckeyes fully expected a shot at what would be Hayes' third title and the school's fourth after they completed an 8-0-1 season by trouncing Michigan 50-20 to claim the championship of the Big Ten. Next up would be the Rose Bowl.

As he arrived at a post-season meeting of the Cleveland booster club as the guest speaker, however, Hayes was informed that the school's faculty council had voted 28-25 not to allow the team to play in the Rose Bowl. Since the conference had no formal pact with the game at the time, the decision meant the team would not make the trip to Pasadena.

Hayes dropped his suitcase, left the building, and went for a 90-minute walk while the crowd waited, expecting to see a formidable display of Hayes' legendary temper. When he returned, however, the coach was calm. He said he didn't agree with the vote,

BUCKEYES

"but I respect their integrity, if not their intelligence."

The athletic board appealed to the school's trustees, who upheld the decision. A chagrined Dick Larkins, the athletic director, said glumly, "We have no recourse now."

Hayes insisted his team would not protest. Indeed, cocaptains Tom Perdue and Mike Ingram addressed more than one group of protestors, urging them to accept the decision.

The decisions you have made along the way have shaped your life at every pivotal moment. Some decisions you made suddenly and carelessly; some you made carefully and deliberately; some were forced upon you. You may have discovered that some of those spur-of-the-moment decisions have turned out better than your carefully considered ones.

Of all your life's decisions, however, none is more important than one you cannot ignore: What have you done with Jesus? Even in his time, people chose to follow Jesus or to reject him, and nothing has changed; the decision must still be made and nobody can make it for you. Ignoring Jesus won't work either; that is, in fact, a decision, and neither he nor the consequences of your decision will go away.

Carefully considered or spontaneous – how you arrive at a decision for Jesus doesn't matter; all that matters is that you get there.

I still don't understand it. I guess the faculty council didn't think bowl games and academics mixed too well, and they didn't let us go.
-- All-Big Ten halfback Paul Warfield on the '61 Rose-Bowl decision

A decision for Jesus may be spontaneous or considered; what counts is that you make it.

DAY 15

THE INTERVIEW

Read Romans 14: 1-12.

"We will all stand before God's judgment seat. . . . So then, each of us will give an account of himself to God" (vv. 10, 12).

Woody Hayes was so unknown in Columbus that Lassie and an inmate serving a life sentence got more votes than he did in a poll of Buckeye fans picking their next head football coach. One interview changed all that.

When Wes Fesler resigned as Ohio State's head football coach in January 1951, forty candidates applied to replace him. Only eight men made it past the initial screen; Hayes was one of them. He was 38 years old with five years of college coaching behind him, all in Ohio: three at Denison University and two at Miami.

The heavy favorite was Paul Brown, who had coached the Buckeyes from 1941-43 and had won the national title in 1942. He had left Columbus to join the Navy during World War II and then had returned to Ohio to coach the Cleveland Browns after the war.

Alumni, students, and a Columbus newspaper launched a "furious campaign" to bring Brown back. Despite Hayes' years of coaching in Ohio, "no one outside of the Buckeyes' screening committee even know who [Hayes] was." In fact, in a newspaper readers' poll, Brown garnered 83 percent of the votes. Hayes finished behind the school's freshman football coach, Lassie the movie dog, actress Lana Turner, President Harry Truman, and an inmate serving a life sentence in the state penitentiary.

Everything about Hayes' life and Ohio State football changed, though, with one three-hour interview. Hayes didn't wait for questions from the committee; he lit right in, telling them why he wanted the job and why he could handle it. He discussed recruiting, hard work, and academics.

Hayes left confident he had done his best and had made a good impression. He had. Despite continued pressure to hire Brown, Hayes was named OSU's nineteenth head football coach.

You know all about job interviews. You've experienced the stress, the anxiety, the helpless feeling that's part of any interview. You tried to appear calm and relaxed while struggling to come up with reasonably original answers to banal questions and to hide your considered opinion that the interviewer was a total geek. You told yourself that if they turned you down, it was their loss.

You won't be so indifferent or nonchalant, though, about your last interview: the one with God. A day will come when we will all stand uncomfortably before God to account for ourselves. It is to God and God alone – not our friends, not our parents, not society in general – that we must give a final and complete account.

Since all eternity will be at stake, it sure would help to have a surefire reference with you. One – and only one -- is available: Jesus Christ.

Gentlemen, I guess the hay is in the barn.
        -- Woody Hayes at the conclusion of his job interview

You will have one last interview -- with God
-- and you sure want Jesus there with you
as a character witness.

OHIO STATE

DAY 16

HANGING IN THERE

Read Mark 14:32-42.

"'Father,' he said, 'everything is possible for you. Take this cup from me. Yet not what I will, but what you will'" (v. 36).

Eddie Days' persistence lasted through four seasons and 33 games of that final year. It finally paid off.

Days was a high school star but received scholarship offers only from smaller schools. His dream was to play for Ohio State, so he walked on as a freshman in the fall of 2007. He made the squad. But he had a heart condition, and team doctors ran him through a battery of tests. By the time they cleared him to play, the roster was full. "That was really devastating," said his mom.

But Days hung in there. He stayed in shape and even helped the women's basketball team practice. The next year, though, the roster was full and the team didn't hold tryouts. The following year tryouts were held, but no one was taken.

Days had now persisted through three years, and he wasn't where he wanted to be. Still, he refused to give up. His mother asked him if it weren't time he gave up playing and considered coaching instead. "No, I want to play," Days replied.

In 2010, for the fourth straight year, Days tried out for the team. This time he made it. He didn't play very much, appearing in only nine games through the season and averaging fewer than two minutes per appearance. He was a practice player, and he loved it.

BUCKEYES

Then on March 20, 2011, with about three minutes left in the 31-1 Buckeyes' 98-66 slaughter of George Mason in the second round of the NCAA Tournament, Ohio State fans started chanting Days' name. Head coach Thad Matta put him in.

He was fouled at the end of the game and went to the foul line. In front of his hometown folks and many of his family members, the persistent Eddie Days hit one of two free throws. He had scored what would be the only point of his collegiate career.

"For me, (the free throw) felt like 20 points," his mother said.

Life is tough; it inevitably beats us up and kicks us around some. But life has four quarters, and so here we are, still standing, still in the game. Like Eddie Days and his persistence, we know that we can never win if we don't finish. We emerge as winners and champions only if we never give up, if we just see it through.

Interestingly, Jesus has been in the same situation. On that awful night in the garden, Jesus understood the nature of the suffering he was about to undergo, and he begged God to take it from him. In the end, though, he yielded to God's will and surrendered his own.

Even in the matter of persistence, Jesus is our example. As he did, we push doggedly and determinedly ahead – following God's will for our lives -- no matter how hard it gets. And we can do it because God is with us.

It finally worked out.
– Eddie Days on making the team his senior year

It's tough to keep going no matter what,
but you have the power of almighty
God to pull you through.

DAY 17

CALLING IT QUITS

Read Numbers 13:25-14:4.

"The men who had gone up with him said, 'We can't attack those people; they are stronger than we are'" (v. 13:31).

I'm outta here. I'm going to West Virginia to play." So declared one of the greatest players in Ohio State history right after Woody Hayes threw him off the team.

Jim Stillwagon was one of the "Super Sophomores" of 1968 who went undefeated and won the national title. He started at middle guard for three seasons and was All-America in 1969 and '70. He won the Outland Trophy and the Lombardi Award in 1970 as the nation's best lineman and is a member of both the OSU Athletics Hall of Fame and the College Football Hall of Fame.

In the fall of '68, though, Stillwagon was unproven. As Joe Menzer tells it, in practice he flattened quarterback Rex Kern, a fellow super soph whom Hayes had already chosen as his starter. Kern was wearing a yellow jersey at the time, which signified that defensive players were not to touch him.

The legendary Hayes temper erupted as he ripped into Still-wagon, who replied that he was just trying to get to the guy with the ball. "Get this guy out of here!" Hayes bellowed at some security guards. "We're taking your scholarship away, son."

Stillwagon had a few choice words for the coach before he was escorted off the field. His intention was to keep going, right

BUCKEYES

off campus. Assistant coach Bill Mallory stopped by the locker room to calm him down. That's when Stillwagon insisted he was quitting the team and the school to play for West Virginia.

"Woody will cool off and everything will be fine," Mallory said. "I don't care," Stillwagon replied.

When Hayes saw that Kern was fine, he did calm down and urged Stillwagon to stay. He had to pull out his big guns though -- telling Stillwagon his parents would be disappointed in him if he quit Ohio State -- before the stubborn future star agreed to stay.

Remember that time you quit a high-school sports team? Or that night you bailed out of a relationship? Walked away from a job with the goals unachieved? Sometimes quitting is the most sensible way to minimize your losses, so you may well at times in your life give up on something or someone.

In your relationship with God, however, you should remember the people of Israel, who quit when the Promised Land was theirs for the taking. They forgot one fact of life you never should: God never gives up on you.

That means you should never, ever give up on God. No matter how tired or discouraged you get, no matter that it seems your prayers aren't getting through to God, no matter what – quitting on God is not an option.

He is preparing a blessing for you, and in his time, he will bring it to fruition -- if you don't quit on him.

He might cool off, but I'm not going to cool off. I'm leaving.
— Jim Stillwagon to coach Bill Mallory

Whatever else you give up on in your life, don't give up on God; he will never ever give up on you.

DAY 18

BIG DEAL

Read Ephesians 3:1-13.

"His intent was that now, through the church, the manifold wisdom of God should be made known" (v. 10).

Ohio State football is, of course, a really big deal, but it didn't get that way until one of the program's tiniest players came along.

Twenty-six years after its birth, the OSU football program was coming into its own in 1916. Larger crowds than ever before were coming to the games at Ohio Field, which had first been called University Field. For most games, 5,000 to 7,000 fans were showing up.

Then in 1917, a tiny sophomore "with a big heart and blazing speed" exploded onto the scene and propelled OSU football into the big time. He was Charles W. "Chic" Harley.

Harley stood only 5'9" tall and weighed only 155 pounds, but "he was virtually untouchable in the open field" because he was faster than any other player of the time. He also "possessed the moves and cutting ability of many of today's best running backs."

By mid-season of 1917, Harley "was fast becoming Ohio's first real football hero." As a result, Ohio Field was crammed with more than 12,000 fans for the Wisconsin game.

When Harley returned to Columbus in 1919 after a year's absence because of World War I, 28,000 fans showed up for the Michigan game in Ann Arbor. The Buckeyes won 13-3, and Ohio State officials understood what had happened. Chic Harley had

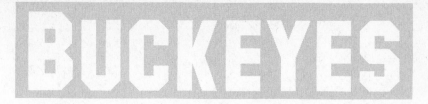

virtually singlehandedly rendered Ohio Field obsolete.

In 1920, the university began raising money to build a new stadium. The groundbreaking was held on Aug. 3, 1921, and Ohio Stadium opened in time for the 1922 season with 71,138 fans showing up for the first game.

The stadium was inevitable, but Harley's talent ignited both the sport's popularity and the push for a larger playpen for the Buckeyes. Chic Harley was a big deal -- and thus so became Ohio State football.

"Big deals" are important components of the unfolding of our lives. Our wedding, childbirth, a new job, a new house, big Buckeye games, even a new car. In many ways, what we regard as a big deal is what shapes not only our lives but our character.

One of the most unfathomable anomalies of faith in America today is that while many people profess to be die-hard Christians, they disdain involvement with a local church. As Paul tells us, however, the Church is a very big deal to God; it is at the heart of his redemptive work; it is a vital part of his eternal purposes.

The Church is no accident of history. It isn't true that Jesus died and all he wound up with for his troubles was the stinking Church. It is no consolation prize.

Rather, the Church is the primary instrument through which God's plan of cosmic and eternal salvation is worked out. And it doesn't get any bigger than that.

Chic Harley put Ohio State football on the map.
-- Archie Griffin

To disdain church involvement is to assert that God doesn't know what he's doing.

DAY 19

FUTURE PERFECT

Read Matthew 6:25-34.

"Do not worry about tomorrow, for tomorrow will worry about itself" (v. 34).

Tyler Moeller couldn't see the future, but he knew something bad was about to happen to him.

The senior defensive back was suiting up for the Illinois game of Oct. 2, 2010, when he felt a tweak on the left side of his chest. For other players, the discomfort would be nothing to worry about. Moeller, however, estimated at the time that since he had first torn his left pectoral muscle in 2008, he had partially torn that same muscle again about a dozen times. He knew the injury had never fully healed and that eventually something big and something bad was going to happen to him.

This was the day.

Moeller had known bad luck before. He missed the 2009 season after he was assaulted while on a family vacation. He hit his head when he fell after being suckerpunched in the face, suffered bleeding in his brain, and spent time in intensive care fighting for his life. His attacker eventually pled guilty to assault.

When doctors suggested Moeller give up football, he refused. "Why would I want to keep playing?" he asked. "Because I love it."

So here he was in 2010, on the field for the 4-0 Buckeyes for Illinois' opening drive. Making a tackle, Moeller felt the muscle rip from the bone. Before the doctors even took a look at the injury,

he knew his fate. "I knew it was totally torn when it happened," he said. "The trainers didn't even have to tell me what was wrong."

Unfortunately, it was as Moeller expected. He had completely torn his left pectoral muscle, sidelining him for yet another season.

Moeller couldn't see into the future clearly enough to know if he would ever play again, but the NCAA granted his appeal for a sixth season of eligibility. He played in every game in 2011, earning an honorable mention nod on the All-Big Ten team.

We worry about many things, but nothing tops the frequency with which we fret about tomorrow because we don't know what it will bring. How would we live if I lost my job? How can we pay for our children's college? What will I do when my parents can't take care of themselves? What will the Buckeyes do next season?

Amid our worries about the future, along comes Jesus to tell us, in effect, "Don't worry. Be happy." Well, that's all right for Jesus, but he never had a mortgage to pay or teenagers in the house.

In telling us how to approach tomorrow, though, Jesus understood a crucial aspect of the future: Your future is determined by how you live in the present. Particularly is this true in your spiritual life. God has carefully planned your eternal future to include unremitting glory, joy, and peace. It's called Heaven.

You must, however, claim that future in the present through faith in Jesus. And then – don't worry about it.

I kind of thought it was a ticking time bomb. Something big was going to happen eventually.
-- Tyler Moeller on his injured pectoral muscle

You lay claim to a sure future
through a present faith in Jesus Christ.

DAY 20

ONE TOUGH COOKIE

Read 2 Corinthians 11:21b-29.

"Besides everything else, I face daily the pressure of my concern for all the churches" (v. 28).

Samantha Prahalis mixed toughness with talent to assemble one of the greatest careers in Buckeye basketball history.

With her typical flair for the dramatic, Prahalis saved her most spectacular performance for the last home game of her Ohio State career. On Feb. 23, 2012, the senior guard set a school single-game record by pouring in 42 points in an 81-56 romp past Minnesota. "You just get hot," she explained.

Only a few days later, Prahalis, who set the all-time Big Ten record for career assists, was named the conference Player of the Year after leading the league in scoring and assists. She joined teammate Tayler Hill on the All-Big Ten first team.

Prahalis played right through the last minute of her career exactly as she had always played the game: with a fiery demeanor and a toughness that fueled some criticism. She had to be tough because, as she explained it, "I don't look like a kid that even plays basketball." She stands only 5'6" and has been described as "a slim white girl with China doll looks."

She was always tough and talented. In the seventh grade, she played on an elite Brooklyn team as the only white player in the game. "Her first practice was as much about the dare as it was basketball."

BUCKEYES

Her father drove her from Long Island to a fenced-in playground basketball court in New York City, "a court dominated by 20-something African-American women." "Here she was," he said, "a 15- or 16-year-old white girl and playing on the cement." They tested her immediately, knocking her down when she shot. "Sammy Prahalis ate cement and popped up for a second helping."

"She's a tough kid," her dad said. And a Buckeye legend.

You don't have to be a legendary Ohio State basketball player like Samantha Prahalis to be tough. In America today, toughness isn't restricted to physical accomplishments and brute strength. Going to work every morning even when you feel bad, sticking by your rules for your children in a society that ridicules parental authority, making hard decisions about your aging parents' care often over their objections — you've got to be tough every day just to live honorably, decently, and justly.

Living faithfully requires toughness too, though in America chances are you won't be imprisoned, stoned, or flogged this week for your faith as Paul was. Still, contemporary society exerts subtle, psychological, daily pressures on you to turn your back on your faith and your values. Popular culture promotes promiscuity, atheism, and gutter language; your children's schools have kicked God out; the corporate culture advocates amorality before the shrine of the almighty dollar.

You have to hang tough to keep the faith.

I like tough, honest people.

— Woody Hayes

Life demands more than mere physical toughness; you must be spiritually tough too.

DAY 21

TRICK PLAYS

Read Acts 19:11-20.

"The evil spirit answered them, 'Jesus I know, and I know about Paul, but who are you?'" (v. 15)

Buckeye quarterback Stan Pincura once pulled a trick on his teammates, his coaches, and the whole Ohio Stadium crowd.

The Ohio State teams of the 1930s were well stocked with real characters. For instance, in 1938 junior Ross Bartschy, a three-year football letterman who also lettered in golf in 1940, was benched for the Northwestern game after he missed his assignment on a punt return the week before. Head coach Francis Schmidt always sat on the end of the bench, and Bartschy purposefully sat down beside him. He kept jabbing the coach in the ribs, asking him to put him in the game, and denigrating the play of his replacement.

By the third quarter, an exasperated Schmidt got up and went to the other end of the bench. He must have thought it over for a moment, though, because he soon strode back to Bartschy and told him, "I am coach of this team. *You* go down to the other end of this bench!"

Pincura lettered for three seasons (1933-35) at Ohio State and went on to play professionally for the Cleveland Rams for two seasons. In 1937, he became a charter member of a new organization called the National Football League.

The custom at OSU games in those days was to shoot off a gun to signal the end of each quarter. In one game, Pincura was

BUCKEYES

trotting into the game from the sideline when an official fired the gun to end the period. Pincura suddenly "grabbed his heart, twirled around a few times, and fell to the ground. The crowd was stunned. They thought he had been shot."

A shocked team trainer, Tucker Smith, and his aides hurried onto the field to tend to the fallen Buckeye. "Are you OK?" Smith asked as he stood over the prone Pincura. "I am OK," the jokester replied. "But how's the crowd taking it?"

Scam artists are everywhere — and they love to try to fool us with their trick plays. An e-mail encourages you to send money to some foreign country to get rich. A guy at your front door offers to resurface your driveway at a ridiculously low price. A TV ad promises a pill to help you lose weight without diet or exercise.

You've been around; you check things out before deciding. The same approach is necessary with spiritual matters, too, because false religions and bogus Christian denominations abound. The key is what any group does with Jesus. Is he the son of God, the ruler of the universe, and the only way to salvation? If not, then what the group espouses is something other than the true Word of God.

The good news about Jesus does indeed sound too good to be true. But the only catch is that there is no catch. No trick -- just the truth.

When you run trick plays and they work, you're a genius. But when they don't work, folks question your sanity.
                                                                        -- Bobby Bowden

**God's promises through Jesus sound too good to
be true, but the only catch is that there is no catch.**

DAY 22

A CHANGE OF PLANS

Read Genesis 18:20-33.

"The Lord said, 'If I find fifty righteous people in the city of Sodom, I will spare the whole place for their sake'" (v. 26).

Mike Doss had his five-year plan all mapped out -- and then Ohio State happened.

Doss capped off a sensational career in Columbus as a star on the 2002 national championship team. The strong safety was the Big Ten Defensive Player of the Year and the MVP of the Fiesta Bowl. For the third straight season, he was named both first-team All-Big Ten and first-team All-America.

But that 2002 season wasn't in his plans.

The one constant in Doss' life growing up was money: There was never enough. He lived with an uncle, and following a phone conversation with his mother his sophomore year of high school, he drew up what he called his five-year plan. It was pretty simple: After his junior year at a big-time college, he would bolt to the NFL and its riches. By the summer of 2002, his mother would be comfortably nestled with a home of her own in the suburbs.

But Doss' five-year plan began to fall apart in December 2001. Ohio State had finished the season a disappointing 7-5, and he was nagged by the thought that his business in Columbus was unfinished. Plus, he was simply having the best time of his life.

The day before the Jan. 11 deadline to declare for the NFL draft,

Doss called family, friends, and pro scouts. His mother told him, "You do what's best for you, son. I can hold on another year." When Doss headed toward the lectern at a press conference the next day, he still didn't know what he was going to do, so he decided to leave it in God's hands. He announced he would return.

Doss' plan simply changed into a six-year one. He was drafted in the second round in 2003 and received a $1.1 million bonus for signing with the Indianapolis Colts.

To be unable to adapt to changing circumstances to is stultify and die. It's true of animal life, of business and industry, of the military, of sports teams, of you and your relationships, your job, and your finances.

Changing your plans regularly therefore is rather routine for you as it turned out to be for Mike Doss. But consider how remark-able it is that the God of the universe may change his mind about something. What could bring that about? Prayer. Someone -- an old nomad named Abraham or a 21st-century OSU fan like you -- talks to God, who listens and considers what is asked of him.

You may feel uncomfortable praying. Maybe you're reluctant and embarrassed; perhaps you feel you're not very good at it. But nobody majors in prayer at school, and as for being reluctant, what have you got to lose? Your answer may even be a change of plans on God's part. Such is the power of prayer.

It started to get to me that I had never helped my team win a title. I felt like there was more for me to do at Ohio State.
-- Mike Doss on why he changed his five-year plan

Prayer is so powerful
that it may even change God's mind.

DAY 23

POWER PLAY

Read Psalm 28.

"The Lord is my strength and my shield; my heart trusts in him, and I am helped" (v. 7a).

The moment of truth had come for the Buckeyes in the volleyball national championship match. Right then and there, they knew they would win it because they were the stronger team.

Ohio State was the ultimate volleyball bridesmaid. Seventeen times the team had been to the final four and had never won the title. The 1969 team went 24-0, but there was no national tournament then. The 2000 team lost in the national title game.

So here they were again in the 2011 national finals against UC Santa Barbara. They started out tight, making nine service errors in a loss in the first set. They regrouped to win the second set 25-20, highlighted by a 12-4 run that featured four kills from Shawn Sangrey. The Buckeyes then stood on the cusp of the coveted title by winning the second set 25-19. They then struggled again, losing the fourth set, to force a winner-take-all race to 15 points.

As they prepared for that tension-filled set, head coach Pete Hanson gathered his team about him. He reminded them they had been there before. Back in February, the Buckeyes had faced UC Irvine in a deciding fifth game and had beaten them. "We kind of looked at [UC Irvine's] team" that night, Hanson said, "and everybody to a man said, 'You know, we're the more physical team right now. We've got more strength that we can bring to the table than those guys across the net.'"

And now with the national title on the line, the Buckeyes had the same moment: They realized they were the stronger team. They went out and showed it, crushing the Gauchos in the fifth game 15-9. They had eleven kills and only one error, playing what Hanson called almost a perfect game offensively.

The stronger team was the 2011 national champion.

You make an honest living in a world that rewards greed and unbridled ambition. You raise your children in a culture that glamorizes immoral behavior and ridicules values and parental authority. You proclaim your faith in a society that idolizes itself.

Standing tall for what you believe may get you admired, but it also makes you a target for the scoffers who fear the depth of your convictions. Living the faithful life thus requires a healthy dose of physical, mental, and emotional strength.

To rely on your own strength, however, is to face the world poorly armed and woefully weak. Count on it: You will fail; the world will inevitably wear you down. Only when you admit your weakness, confess that you need some help, and allow God to be your strength will you prevail.

The strength that undergirds and supports the Christian life is not found in ourselves. Rather, it is found in the power of the Holy Spirit that lives in us.

We just overpowered them.

-- Volleyball coach Pete Hanson

**God did not create us ten feet tall and bulletproof,
so he lends us his own power
to strengthen us in our faith walk.**

UNBELIEVABLE!

Read Hebrews 3:7-19.

*"See to it, brothers, that none of you has a sinful,
unbelieving heart that turns away from the living God"
(v. 12).*

The Michigan band performing Script Ohio -- first. Orange and black uniforms. A bovine homecoming queen. Unbelievable!

Writer Jeff Rapp has declared that documentation exists proving the Wolverine band performed Script Ohio at the OSU-Michigan game of 1932. OSU's Department of Music had asked visiting bands to create a salute to Ohio State to help celebrate the ten-year anniversary of Ohio Stadium. Script Ohio was the salute of the Michigan band. UM music personnel then gave the formation's charts to the OSU band director after that 1932 game.

The Buckeyes in orange and black uniforms? Hard to believe and definitely unimaginable. Yet, when three Ohio State students decided on the school colors in 1878, they picked orange and black. School powers-that-be instructed them to go back to the drawing board because Princeton already had that same combination. On their second try, the guys came up with scarlet and gray, declaring it to be "a pleasing combination."

It's rather unbelievable, but Ohio State's homecoming queen in 1926 was a cow. A group of students decided to pull off one of the greatest pranks in college history and succeeded in getting "Maudine Ormsby" on the ballot. She was a prize-winning Holstein who -- not surprisingly -- drew the wholehearted support of the College of Agriculture. In what is surely the most crooked student election in the school's history, 13,000 ballots were cast -- when the school had only 9,000 students. Maudine won easily. As tradition required, the homecoming queen rode on her own float in the homecoming parade, though her chaperones said she was too young (3) to participate in all the homecoming activities.

Despite ample evidence to their veracity, we may still choose to discount the truth of these three stories. In our lives, what we choose not to believe in reveals much about us. UFOs. Global warming. Sasquatch. Aluminum baseball bats.

Most of what passes for our unbelief has little effect on our lives. Does it matter much that we don't believe a Ginsu knife can stay sharp after repeatedly slicing through tin cans?

That's not the case, however, when Jesus and God are part of the mix. Quite unbelievably, we often hear people blithely assert they don't believe in God. Or brazenly declare they believe in God but don't believe Jesus was anything but a good man and a great teacher.

At this point, unbelief becomes dangerous because God doesn't fool around with scoffers. He locks them out of the Promised Land, which isn't a country in the Middle East but Heaven itself.

Given that scenario, it's downright unbelievable that anyone would not believe.

Football is so incredible sometimes it's unbelievable.

                                                            -- Tom Landry

Perhaps nothing is as unbelievable as that some people insist on not believing in God or his son.

DAY 25

THE LEADER

Read Matthew 16:18-23.

*"You are Peter, and on this rock I will build my church,
and the gates of Hades will not overcome it" (v. 18).*

Leslie Horvath was a star, Ohio State's first Heisman Trophy winner (1944), but he was also his team's unquestioned leader.

Horvath played quarterback and halfback for State in 1940, '41, and '42. After he graduated in '42, he moved on to dentistry school and spent 1943 in an army specialized training program. When Horvath was discharged in 1944, head football coach Carroll Widdoes asked him to come back to the team because of the shortage of players resulting from the war. Horvath turned down some professional offers to play another year with the Buckeyes.

Despite being the lightest regular on the team, the 24-year-old played 402 minutes of football that season, a full quarter more than any of his teammates. He averaged nearly six yards a carry and led the team in scoring.

Surrounded by young players, Horvath's leadership skills were as important as his physical talents as he led the Buckeyes to a 9-0 season and the Big Ten championship. Nowhere was his leadership on display more than in the showdown with Michigan.

As has happened so often over the years, the two teams met with the Big Ten title on the line. With eight minutes on the clock, Michigan led 14-12, but Ohio State got the ball. In keeping with the most storied of football legends, Horvath gathered his young teammates around him before he called the play. He told them, "We are not going to pass. We are not going to fumble. We are not going to give up the ball. We are going right in with a series of first downs. Now, everyone block as he has never blocked before."

The result was exactly what the team's leader ordered, a game-winning drive all on the ground for an 18-14 win.

Every aspect of life that involves people – every organization, every group, every project, every Buckeye team -- must have a leader. If goals are to be reached, somebody must take charge.

Even the early Christian church was no different. Jesus knew this, so he designated the leader in Simon Peter, who was such an unlikely choice to assume such an awesome, world-changing responsibility that Jesus soon after rebuked him as "Satan."

In *Twelve Ordinary Men*, John MacArthur described Simon as "ambivalent, vacillating, impulsive, unsubmissive." Hardly a man to inspire confidence in his leadership skills. Yet, according to MacArthur, Peter became "the greatest preacher among the apostles" and the "dominant figure" in the birth of the church.

The implication for your own life is both obvious and unsettling. You may think you lack the attributes necessary to make a good leader for Christ. But consider Simon Peter, an ordinary man who allowed Christ to rule his life and became the foundation upon which the Christian church was built.

[Leslie] Horvath had the personality and quality of leadership to inspire his mates to almost unbelievable achievements.
-- Former Buckeye Sports Information Director Wilbur Snypp

**God's leaders are men and women
who allow Jesus to lead them.**

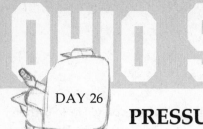

PRESSURE POINT

Read 1 Kings 18:16-40.

"Answer me, O Lord, answer me, so these people will know that you, O Lord, are God" (v. 37).

When junior running back Beanie Wells delivered a message to Terrelle Pryor, the freshman quarterback's only thought was "Don't pressure me anymore."

An ESPN analyst had said Pryor wasn't ready for "a stage this vast." That stage was Camp Randall Stadium on Oct. 4, 2008, when the 14th-ranked Buckeyes took on the 18th-ranked Wisconsin Badgers. Making his first start in a prime-time road-game, Pryor made the analyst look like a prophet most of the night.

"I made some young passes, and I did some young things," Pryor said after the game. Wisconsin did what teams do to a young quarterback: They mixed it up on defense, forcing him into "an agony of indecision." Inevitably, "the stage had dwarfed the freshman." The pressure had just been too much.

The result was a 17-13 Wisconsin lead with 6:31 left on the clock and the Buckeyes sitting at their own 20. The stadium was rocking "as the Buckeyes reeled." "Big drive," was all head coach Jim Tressel said to his young quarterback before he took the field.

It didn't look good. "Rattled like his teammates never expected him to be," Pryor "had played like a freshman" most of the night. He couldn't play like one now, and when Pryor joined the huddle, Wells spoke up and told him so.

BUCKEYES

"This is a man's world," Wells told him. In other words, pressure or no, it was time for Pryor to step up. He did.

He hit Brian Hartline for 19 yards and for 27 and then found Ray Small over the middle for 13 more. In 11 plays, he moved the Buckeyes to the Wisconsin 11 with 68 seconds left.

The freshman then made his most pressure-packed decision of the night. He ran the option to the left side and decided to forgo the pitch to Wells. It was the right move. He scored, and the Buckeyes had a 20-17 win with a last-gasp, pressure-filled drive.

You live every day with pressure. As Elijah did so long ago, you lay it on the line with everybody watching. Your family, coworkers, or employees – they depend on you. You know the pressure of a deadline, of a job evaluation, of taking the risk of asking someone to go out with you, of driving in rush-hour traffic.

Help in dealing with daily pressure is readily available, and the only price you pay for it is your willingness to believe. God will give you the grace to persevere if you ask prayerfully.

And while you may need some convincing, the pressures of daily living are really small potatoes since they all will pass. The real pressure comes when you stare into the face of eternity because what you do with it is irrevocable and forever. You can handle that pressure easily enough by deciding for Jesus. Eternity is then taken care of; the pressure's off – forever.

We put it on [Pryor's] back and we knew he was capable of doing it.
-- Cornerback Malcolm Jenkins on the game-winning drive

The greatest pressure you face in life
concerns where you will spend eternity,
which can be dealt with by deciding for Jesus.

GOOD-BYE

Read John 13:33-38.

"My children, I will be with you only a little longer" (v. 33a).

Courtney Pruner didn't get a chance to say good-bye to her mother. And then again, maybe she did; it just took a while.

Pruner was a standout outfielder-pitcher for the Ohio State softball team who was a two-time All-Big Ten selection and a two-time team captain. Her career took off with an exceptional sophomore season in 2007. She hit .336 and was All-Big Ten; her 37 RBIs were the fifth best in Buckeye history.

But Pruner's right hip was basically falling apart. She was in chronic pain, and eventually her hip would snap every time she took a step. She had two surgeries after that sophomore year and was redshirted for the 2008 season.

On March 21, Pruner was in the doctor's office for a visit after her second surgery when her father called. He spoke four words that turned her world upside down: "Your mom passed away." Two weeks before, her mother had had a stroke. Pruner had gone home for a week before returning to campus because her mother was so much better. "I didn't get to say good-bye," she later said.

As it turned out, Pruner regarded her injuries "as a blessing in disguise because I don't think I would have been able to travel with the team." She just wasn't ready to take the field knowing her mother wouldn't be there to watch her.

BUCKEYES

She came back in 2009 and hit a double in her first at-bat. Not until March 21, though, in the 24th game of the season, did the team have a home game in new Buckeye Field. In her final at bat, she hit a home run, the first one in the new facility. "I couldn't even hold back the tears running around the bases," she said. "I don't even know how to explain it."

Perhaps she was saying good-bye. It was a year to the day her mother had died.

You've stood on the curb and watched someone you love drive off, or you've grabbed a last-minute hug before a plane leaves. Maybe it was a child leaving home for the first time or your best friends moving halfway across the country. Or maybe you've experienced the permanent separation of death. Good-byes hurt.

Jesus felt the pain of parting too. Throughout his brief ministry, Jesus had been surrounded by and had depended upon his friends and confidants, the disciples. About to leave them, he gathered them for a going-away supper and gave them a heads-up about what was about to happen. In the process, he offered them words of comfort. What a wonderful friend he was! Even though he was the one who was about to suffer unimaginable agony, Jesus' concern was for the pain his friends would feel.

But Jesus wasn't just saying good-bye. He was on his mission of providing the way through which none of us would ever have to say good-bye again.

Courtney hit one to heaven.

— OSU softball coach Linda Kalafatis

**Through Jesus, we will see the day
when we say good-bye to goodbyes.**

DAY 28

FEAR FACTOR

Read Matthew 14:22-33.

"[The disciples] cried out in fear. But Jesus immediately said to them: 'Take courage! It is I. Don't be afraid'" (vv. 26-27).

When you're afraid the runway might not be safe for a team plane, what do you do? If you're Woody Hayes, you send in the reserves.

Writer Jeff Snook relates that All-American Buckeye receiver Terry Glenn was afraid of flying. He simply refused to set foot on a plane. A former walk-on, Glenn won the Fred Biletnikoff Award as the nation's top receiver in his senior season of 1995. He rarely traveled with the team to away games, though. Instead, he drove, often arriving late on a Friday night and thus playing the next day with less sleep than his teammates.

Glenn wasn't the first apparently fearless Buckeye player to be afraid of flying. Jim Parker was an offensive lineman who was All-America in 1955 and '56, won the Outland Trophy as college football's best interior lineman, and was inducted into the Pro Football Hall of Fame in 1973 and the College Football Hall of Fame in 1974. "I didn't like to fly," he admitted. "You almost had to hypnotize me to get me on an airplane." His fear never evaporated, even during a long pro career. At Ohio State, Parker always watched to see which plane Hayes boarded and then got on that one.

His approach was probably a good one as an incident in 1976

BUCKEYES

indicates. At the time, the airport at State College, home of Penn State, had runways so short that the team had to use two smaller planes, dubbed Red One and Red Two, rather than one larger craft that could accommodate the whole team.

Red One carried Hayes, his assistant coaches, and the starters while Red Two flew reserve players and some school personnel. When the pilot of Red One told Hayes he wasn't sure of the safety standards for the airport runway, the coach told him, "Send in Red Two. If they make it, then we'll go in."

Some fears are universal; others are particular. Speaking to the Rotary Club may require a heavy dose of antiperspirant. Elevator walls may feel as though they're closing in on you. And don't even get started on being in the dark with spiders and snakes during a thunderstorm.

We all live in fear, and God knows this. Dozens of passages in the Bible urge us not to be afraid. God isn't telling us to lose our wariness of oncoming cars or big dogs with nasty dispositions; this is a helpful fear God instilled in us for protection.

What God does wish driven from our lives is a spirit of fear that dominates us, that makes our lives miserable and keeps us from doing what we should, such as sharing our faith. In commanding that we not be afraid, God reminds us that when we trust completely in him, we find peace that calms our fears.

I am not flying. Can't do it. Don't ask me.

— *Terry Glenn*

**You have your own peculiar set of fears,
but they should never paralyze you because
God is greater than anything you fear.**

DAY 29

PRAYER WARRIORS

Read Luke 18:1-8.

"Then Jesus told his disciples a parable to show them that they should always pray and not give up" (v. 1).

Sophomore cornerback Dustin Fox spent some time in prayer before the 2003 Fiesta Bowl. His prayers were answered.

Much of the hype leading up to the BCS national title game of 2003 centered on the contrasting styles of the Buckeyes and the Miami Hurricanes. Ohio State's offense was "one of the least prolific in the Big Ten"; while the Buckeyes liked to feature freshman tailback Maurice Clarett and run the ball, the Canes used the run to set up the pass. Their offense ranked in the top 10 in most categories, and that explosive offense was what had Fox praying. Pregame talk said it was coming right his way.

It made sense. The Hurricanes were clearly not interested in attacking star Buckeye defenders Mike Doss and Chris Gamble. Next to them, Fox was the secondary's weakest link; thus, he would be easier to exploit.

Senior free safety Donnie Nickey wasn't buying it. "All that about [Fox[being the weak link came from the media," he said. "He's made plays . . . all year long. That's why he's out there."

Fox's prayers were indeed answered. He didn't look anything like a weak link as he made two big plays that helped his team to the 31-24 win over Miami.

Fox's first big play came in the second quarter. Miami had a 7-

BUCKEYES

0 lead and was moving again when Fox nabbed a pick at midfield. The play helped turn some of the game's momentum OSU's way.

His second clutch play came late in the fourth quarter with Miami leading 17-14 and on their way to what could well have been a game-clinching touchdown. On a pass completion, Fox stripped the ball, and junior free safety Will Allen claimed it at the Ohio State 18.

Before and during the game, Dustin Fox did exactly what Jesus taught us to do as his followers: always pray and never give up.

Any problems we may have with prayer and its results derive from our side, not God's. We pray for a while about something – perhaps fervently at first – but our enthusiasm wanes if we don't receive the answer we want exactly when we want it. Why waste our time by asking for the same thing over and over again?

But God isn't deaf; God does hear our prayers, and God does respond to them. As Jesus clearly taught, our prayers have an impact because they turn the power of Almighty God loose in this world. Thus, falling to our knees and praying to God is not a sign of weakness and helplessness. Rather, praying for someone or something is an aggressive act, an intentional ministry, a conscious and fervent attempt on our part to change someone's life or the world for the better.

God responds to our prayers; we often just can't perceive or don't understand how he is working to make those prayers come about.

I was praying before the game to make a few plays and help the team.
                                    -- Dustin Fox on the BCS title game

Jesus taught us to always pray and never give up.

DAY 30

FAMILY TIES

Read Mark 3:31-35.

"[Jesus] said, 'Here are my mother and my brothers! Whoever does God's will is my brother and sister and mother'" (vv. 34-35).

George Jacoby and his wife, Nina, were such a part of the Hayes family that Annie Hayes would often tell people that her "husband got into bed with [Jacoby's] pregnant wife."

Jacoby was an All-Big Ten tackle in 1952 and '53. He was MVP of the '52 team and cocaptain of the '53 squad.

After Jacoby's freshman season, Hayes asked why his grades were falling down. Jacoby replied that he was going home on the weekends to see his girlfriend. "Why don't you marry her and bring her down here?" the coach asked. Jacoby did.

The couple virtually became part of the Hayes family, even doing their laundry at the coach's home. Nina would often come to practice where Hayes would wink and nod toward the bench, which meant she could stay.

Hayes once had the Jacobys stash recruit Hubert Bobo in their apartment to keep other schools away from him. Jacoby said, "Nina was up all night long, checking to make sure nobody got to Hubie, but we got him signed."

After Jacoby graduated and the couple returned for a home game, they stopped by to see Annie Hayes. Nina was pregnant with their first son, and Mrs. Hayes refused to let them leave. She

BUCKEYES

told them to take one of her husband's double beds. "Don't worry about it," she said. "Woody watches film all night, and he won't be home until about 6:00 in the morning."

Sure enough, Hayes came into the bedroom early in the morning when it was still dark and sat down on a bed. "George, Woody's here. He's on the end of the bed," Nina said. When Jacoby called the coach's name, he bellowed, "Jacoby, what are you doing here?"

Thoroughly amused, Annie Hayes for years told people about the time her husband got into bed with a pregnant Nina Jacoby.

Some wit said families are like fudge, mostly sweet with a few nuts. You can probably call the names of your sweetest relatives, whom you cherish, and of the nutty ones too, whom you mostly try to avoid at a family reunion.

Like it or not, you have a family, and that's God's doing. God cherishes the family so much that he chose to live in one as a son, a brother, and a cousin.

One of Jesus' more startling actions was to redefine the family. No longer is it a single household of blood relatives or even a clan or a tribe. Jesus' family is the result not of an accident of birth but rather a conscious choice. All those who do God's will are members of Jesus' family.

What a startling and downright wonderful thought! You have family members out there you don't even know who stand ready to love you just because you're part of God's family.

Coach would tell our boys how important it was to get a good education.
-- George Jacoby on practically being part of the Hayes family

**For followers of Jesus, family comes not from
a shared ancestry but from a shared faith.**

DAY 31

A LONG SHOT

Read Matthew 9:9-13.

"[Jesus] saw a man named Matthew sitting at the tax collector's booth. 'Follow me,' he told him, and Matthew got up and followed him" (v. 9).

Nobody saw this coming." That's how much of a long shot the Buckeyes were against Michigan State.

As the Ohio State men's basketball team prepared for the last regular-season game against Michigan State on March 4, 2012, "by all appearances, [they] were fading." They had been ranked No. 2 in the nation when they entered the conference schedule, but even head coach Thad Matta acknowledged that the league season had not "gone as well as everybody on the outside thought."

The team lost twice early on but seemed to right itself with six straight conference wins before dropping three straight to fellow contenders. An irate and frustrated Matta even threw the whole bunch out of practice one day.

The pundits declared, "There was no way Ohio State could win the finale." Several factors rendered the Buckeyes long shots: 1) the game was on the road; 2) it was Senior Day; 3) the Spartans could win the Big Ten title outright with a win; 4) they had hammered the Buckeyes in Columbus less than a month earlier.

Yet, there the long shots were, tied with the 5th-ranked Spartans at 70 with 24.7 seconds left. The place was so noisy and so berserk that ear plugs had been handed out along press row.

BUCKEYES

Matta drew up a play that featured a backup plan. The Spartan defense forced the Buckeyes to go to it. Point guard Aaron Craft got the ball to fellow guard William Buford, the team's only senior. He dribbled twice and drained a 20-foot jumper with one second remaining for the 72-70 win.

The long shots had made up two games on the Spartans in the final week of the regular season and had gained a share of their third straight Big Ten title, their fifth in the last seven seasons.

Like the Buckeyes against Michigan State, Matthew the tax collector was a long shot, an unlikely person to be a confidant of the Son of God. While we may not get all warm and fuzzy about the IRS, our government's revenue agents are nothing like Matthew and his ilk. He bought a franchise, paying the Roman Empire for the privilege of extorting, bullying, and stealing everything he could from his own people. Tax collectors of the time were "despicable, vile, unprincipled scoundrels."

And yet, Jesus said only two words to this lowlife: "Follow me." Jesus knew that this long shot would make an excellent disciple.

It's the same with us. While we may not be quite as vile as Matthew was, none of us can stand before God with our hands clean and our hearts pure. We are all impossibly long shots to enter God's Heaven. That is, until we do what Matthew did: get up and follow Jesus.

Through it all, I've seen this team continue to fight.
-- Thad Matta on how the long shots beat Michigan State

Only through Jesus does our status change
from being long shots to enter God's Kingdom
to being heavy favorites.

DAY 32

FATHERS AND SONS

Read Luke 3:1-22.

"And a voice came from heaven: 'You are my Son, whom I love; with you I am well pleased'" (v. 22).

Archie Griffin came home from a recruiting visit with Woody Hayes feeling Ohio State wasn't really interested in him -- and then his dad straightened him out.

Griffin, of course, is a Buckeye icon of whom it has been said, he "holds a status akin to a living folk hero." He is the only player to win the Heisman Trophy twice. He led the Buckeyes in rushing all four seasons (1972-75), and his total of 5,589 career rushing yards was at the time an NCAA record. He was enshrined in the College Football Hall of Fame in 1986.

The greatest running back in Buckeye history actually started his football career on the offensive line and at nose guard and played little his first two years of organized ball. In the seventh grade, though, his team's fullback didn't show up for the first practice, and Griffin volunteered to step in. One of the game's greatest careers was on its way.

When Griffin visited the Ohio State campus on a recruiting trip his senior year, Hayes spent three hours in a restaurant talking to him. That meeting apparently left the young man somewhat dazed and confused.

When Griffin got home, he told his dad he didn't think Coach Hayes wanted him to play for Ohio State. His father asked him why. "Well," the son replied, "the whole time I was there we never talked about football. He wanted to talk about other things, mostly my academics." James Griffin's response was succinct. "Son," he said, "you go play football for that man."

Dad spoke; son listened. The rest, of course, is Buckeye legend.

Contemporary American society largely belittles and marginalizes fathers and their influence upon their sons. Men are perceived as necessary to effect pregnancy; after that, they can just leave and everybody's better off.

But we need look in only two places to appreciate the enormity of that misconception: our jails – packed with males who lacked the influence of fathers in their lives as they grew up -- and the Bible. God – being God – could have chosen any relationship he desired between Jesus and himself, including society's approach of irrelevancy.

Instead, the most important relationship in all of history was that of father-son. God obviously believes a close, loving relationship between fathers and sons, such as that of James and Archie Griffin, is crucial. For men and women to espouse otherwise or for men to walk blithely and carelessly out of the lives of their children constitutes disobedience to the divine will.

Simply put, God loves fathers. After all, he is one.

My dad was a huge influence on me. I imagine if he had put a wrench in my hand I would have been a great mechanic.
-- Pete Maravich

**Fatherhood is a tough job, but a mode
for the father-child relationship is found
in that of Jesus the Son with God the Father.**

BAD IDEA

Read Mark 14:43-50.

*"The betrayer had arranged a signal with them: 'The one
I kiss is the man; arrest him and lead him away under
guard'" (v. 44).*

Woody Hayes once had an idea so bad that it nearly cost him
both his quarterback for the Rose Bowl and a realistic shot at the
national title.

All that stood between the 1968 Buckeyes "and the immor-
tality of an unbeaten season and [a] national championship" was
second-ranked Southern California in the Rose Bowl. Hayes
pushed his team hard, duplicating the California heat they would
endure by practicing indoors and bringing in a bunch of portable
heaters to crank the temperature up to 90 degrees. He also had the
bright idea that the quarterbacks should hit the tackling dummy.
"Fired up and not knowing any better," recalled Rex Kern, "we
ran over to Woody and got ready to hit the tackling dummy."

As the starter, Kern was first in line. Wilbur Snypp and Bob
Hunter wrote, "Why Rex Kern was not a consensus all-American
in at least one of his three years as an Ohio State quarterback is a
question often asked." Kern led the Buckeyes to a 27-2 record as
a starter and set the school's single-season total offense record in
1969 and the career total offense record (both since broken).

So Kern hit the tackling dummy and promptly dropped to the
ground in a heap. When the panicked Hayes ran up, Kern told

him he had dislocated his shoulder. "All right, you quarterbacks," Hayes barked. "That's enough of that for today."

Thankfully, the injury was to Kern's non-throwing shoulder. He played the Rose Bowl with a special harness that left him with limited motion in that arm. Still, he completed 9 of 15 passes for two touchdowns and ran for 35 yards as the Buckeyes won 27-16. Despite Hayes' very bad idea, Kern was the game's MVP.

That sure-fire investment you made from a pal's hot stock tip. The expensive exercise machine that now traps dust bunnies under your bed. Blond hair. Telling your wife you wanted to eat at the restaurant with the waitresses in the skimpy shorts. They seemed like pretty good ideas at the time; they weren't.

We all have bad ideas in our lifetime. They provide some of our most crucial learning experiences. Even Woody Hayes learned he shouldn't have his quarterbacks hitting the tackling dummies.

Some ideas, though, are so irreparably and inherently bad that we cannot help but wonder why they were even conceived in the first place. Almost two thousand years ago a man had just such an idea. Judas' betrayal of Jesus remains to this day one of the most heinous acts of treachery in history.

Turning his back on Jesus was a bad idea for Judas then; it's a bad idea for us now.

Bat Day seems like a good idea, but I question the advisability of giving bats in the Bronx to 40,000 Yankee fans.
— *Cartoonist Aaron Bacall*

**We all have some pretty bad ideas
during our lifetimes, but nothing equals
the folly of turning away from Jesus.**

DAY 34

THE 'I' IN PRIDE

Read 1 John 2:15-17.

"Everything in the world -- the desire of the flesh, the desire of the eyes, the pride in riches -- comes not from the Father but from the world" (v. 16 NRSV).

All Jim Tressel promised was that OSU fans would be proud of their football team. What they heard, however, was a guarantee of a win over Michigan.

On the evening of Jan. 19, 2001, the day that he was hired as Ohio State's head football coach, Tressel attended the Buckeye basketball game. At halftime, he took a microphone to introduce himself to the crowd. That's when he proclaimed, "I can assure you that you'll be proud of our young people in the classroom, in the community, and, most especially, in 310 days in Ann Arbor, Michigan."

Wide receiver Drew Carter and quarterback Steve Bellisari were among those in the crowd that night who heard a promise. "We looked at each other and were like, 'Wow, this guy really means business,'" Carter said. Then he realized, "I guess now we have to back that statement up."

In understanding Tressel to guarantee a win over Michigan, perhaps Buckeye fans were grabbing at anything they could to feel optimistic. After all, Ohio State had beaten the despised Wolverines only twice in the last thirteen meetings.

From the day Tressel was hired, he focused on the Michigan

BUCKEYES

game. He could recite without hesitation how many days remained until kickoff. Every Saturday during spring practice, he had his team watch a quarter of the loss in 2000.

The Buckeyes made good on their coach's promise whether it involved pride or a victory, knocking Michigan out of the Big Ten title and a Rose Bowl berth with a 26-20 win. "I am so proud of these kids," Tressell said after the game. So were the fans.

What are you most proud of? The size of your bank account? The trophies from your tennis league? The title under your name at the office? Your family?

Pride is one of life's great paradoxes. You certainly want a surgeon who takes pride in her work or a Buckeye coach who is proud of his team's accomplishments. But pride in the things and the people of this world is inevitably disappointing because it leads to dependence upon things that will pass away and idolization of people who will fail you. Self-pride is even more dangerous because it inevitably leads to self-glorification.

Pride in the world's baubles and its people lures you to the earthly and the temporary, and away from God and the eternal. Pride in yourself yields the same results in that you exalt yourself and not God.

God alone is glorious enough to be worshipped. Jesus Christ alone is Lord.

I didn't promise this win. I promised you would be proud of us.
-- Jim Tressel after the 2001 Michigan game

**Pride can be dangerous because it tempts you
to lower your sight from God and the eternal
to the world and the temporary.**

DAY 35

HOME IMPROVEMENT

Read Ephesians 4:7-16.

*"The body of Christ may be built up until we all reach
unity in the faith and in the knowledge of the Son of God
and become mature, attaining to the whole measure of the
fullness of Christ" (vv. 12b, 13).*

Everyone wasn't sure the Buckeyes were improving under their new head coach even though the record said so.

Ohio State went 4-3-2 in 1951, Woody Hayes' first year at the helm. The new coach's relationship with his team was so rocky that the players locked him out of the locker room prior to a game. In an age before athletic scholarships, players earned money by working part-time at local businesses. At season's end, assistant coach Ernie Godfrey told Hayes the downtown folks were so disgruntled that the jobs might be withdrawn. "I'll mortgage my house and pay the players myself!" Hayes thundered.

The Buckeyes improved to 6-3 in 1952, including a 27-7 beating of Michigan, "and the downtown folks backed off a little." Not everyone did, though, as a famous exchange between the crusty coach and a feisty elderly fan illustrates.

Joe Menzer related that after the Michigan game, an older woman approached Hayes and asked him, "What was the score of your Illinois game?" "We won twenty-seven to seven," Hayes replied with not a little pride.

"And what was the score of your Michigan game? she asked.

BUCKEYES

Again, Hayes was proud to report that the Buckeyes won by the same score, 27-7.

The woman snorted in disdain. "You aren't making much of an improvement, are you?" she said and stalked away, leaving the head coach -- for at least once in his life -- speechless.

After another 6-3 season in 1953, Hayes' Buckeyes improved to 10-0 in 1954 and won the Big Ten and the national titles.

Just as the Buckeyes do, you try to improve at whatever you tackle. You attend training sessions and seminars to do your job better. You take golf or tennis lessons and practice to get better. You play that new video game until you master it.

To get better at anything requires a dedication involving practice, training, study, and preparation. Your faith life is no different. Jesus calls us to improve ourselves spiritually by becoming more mature in our faith.

We can always know more about God's word, discover more ways to serve God, deepen our prayer life and our trust in God, and do a better job of being Jesus to other people through simple acts of kindness and caring. In other words, we can always become more like Jesus.

One day we will all stand before God as finished products. We certainly want to present him a mature dwelling, a spiritual mansion, not a hovel.

Every day as a person, you are either getting better or you are getting worse. Which do you want to be?
                                                                  -- Woody Hayes

**Spiritual improvement means a constant effort
to become more like Jesus in our day-to-day lives.**

DAY 36

MEMORY LOSS

Read 1 Corinthians 11:17-29.

"[D]o this in remembrance of me" (v. 24).

Jerry Lucas put his prodigious and downright freaky memory to work for God.

As a sophomore in 1959, Lucas averaged 27 points and 17 rebounds in teaming with John Havlicek to lead the Ohio State basketball team to the national championship. In both 1960 and '61, OSU lost to Cincinnati in the finals. In 1999, *Sports Illustrated* named Lucas to its five-man College All-Century Team. In 1996, the NBA named him one of its fifty greatest players.

As memorable as were Lucas' basketball talents, his memory and his mind tricks have always been even more remarkable. He once memorized the first 500 pages of the Manhattan phone book. While he was on the court both in the NBA and at Ohio State, he kept a running total of all the players' statistics. If given a word, he can spell it aloud instantly with the letters arranged in alphabetical order.

After Lucas walked away from pro basketball when he was 34, he became an educator and memory expert. He cowrote *The Memory Book* and developed the Lucas Learning System, the foundation of which is his belief that through what he calls "automatic learning," anyone can share both his prodigious memory and the ability to learn that it brings.

In his final NBA season of 1973-74, Lucas became a born-again

BUCKEYES

Christian when a friend handed him a Bible and he proceeded to memorize the New Testament. That changed his life, but, he said, "It took me a long time to realize that God was speaking to me."

He took his unique message -- a blend of salvation and Scripture memorization as a path to understanding the Bible -- to churches. He published a guide to committing Scripture to memory called *Remember the Word*.

Ultimately, Jerry Lucas remembered the source of all he had.

Memory makes us who we are. Whether our memories appear as pleasant reverie or unnerving nightmares, they shape us and to a large extent determine both our actions and our reactions. Alzheimer's is so terrifying because it steals our memory from us, and in the process we lose ourselves. We disappear.

The greatest tragedy of our lives is that God remembers. In response to that photographic memory, he condemns us for our sin. Paradoxically, the greatest joy of our lives is that God remembers. In response to that memory, he came as Jesus to wash even the memory of our sins away.

Through memory, we encounter revival. At the Last Supper, Jesus instructed his disciples and us to remember. In sharing this unique meal with fellow believers and remembering Jesus and his actions, we meet Christ again, not just as a memory but as an actual living presence. To remember is to keep our faith alive.

You can't study and understand the Bible without realizing that things in there are life-changing.

-- Jerry Lucas

**Because we remember Jesus,
God will not remember our sins.**

DAY 37

PAYBACK

Read Matthew 5:38-42.

"I tell you, Do not resist an evil person. If someone strikes you on the right cheek, turn to him the other also" (v. 39).

I've been thinking about Michigan every morning when I got up for a whole year." Thus declared Buckeye quarterback Rex Kern -- and what was on his mind was revenge.

In 1969, the Buckeyes "were being hailed as perhaps the greatest team in college football history. They were a juggernaut" and were ranked No. 1 when they rolled into Ann Arbor. And lost in what was billed as "one of the greatest upsets of all time."

Not surprisingly, that loss infuriated Woody Hayes. Inside the locker room after the defeat, the coach told his team, "We will start preparing for those guys on the way back home." "Avenging that loss became his obsession for the next 12 months." He had a custom-stitched rug with the '69 score on it placed outside the dressing room as he passed his obsession on to his players.

In the Thursday practice before the 1970 game, Hayes huddled with his offense, suddenly dropped to his knees, and crawled around on all fours, touching each player's shoes. "I want to feel your feet to see if you're ready," he explained.

The "biggest revenge game in Ohio State history" was a collision of undefeateds for the first time in the history of the series. The Buckeyes led 10-9 as the fourth quarter started. They ran the ball ten straight times on a drive that netted a field goal for a 13-9

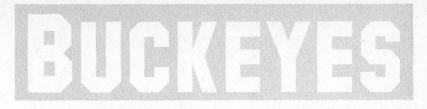

lead with 10:57 left in the game.

On the next series, linebacker Stan White picked off a pass and returned it to the Michigan 9. On third down, Kern ran wide and pitched to halfback Leophus Hayden, who scored untouched.

The 20-9 final was on the board, and Woody Hayes and his Buckeyes had their revenge.

The very nature of an intense rivalry such as Ohio State and Michigan is that the loser will seek payback for the defeat of the season before. But what about in life when somebody's done you wrong; is it time to get even?

The problem with revenge in real-life is that it isn't as clear-cut as a scoreboard. Life is so messy that any attempt at revenge is often inadequate or, worse, backfires and injures you.

As a result, you remain gripped by resentment and anger, which hurts you and no one else. You poison your own happiness while that other person goes blithely about her business. The only way someone who has hurt you can keep hurting you is if you're a willing participant.

But it doesn't have to be that way. Jesus ushered in a new way of living when he taught that we are not to seek revenge for personal wrongs and injuries. Let it go and go on with your life. What a relief!

Going to the Rose Bowl wasn't the main thought on [the players']
minds; it was avenging last year's loss.
-- Woody Hayes after the win over Michigan in 1970

Resentment and anger over a wrong
injures you, not the other person,
so forget it -- just as Jesus taught.

DAY 38

SMART MOVE

Read 1 Kings 4:29-34; 11:1-6.

"[Solomon] was wiser than any other man. . . . As Solomon grew old, his wives turned his heart after other gods, and his heart was not fully devoted to the Lord his God" (vv. 4:31, 11:4).

Quarterback Craig Krenzel had a reputation for brilliance in the classroom even before he made the smart move that resulted in a legendary Buckeye play.

In 2001, when All-American center LeCharles Bentley was told that Krenzel, a sophomore and the third-string QB, would miss a game to attend his sister's wedding, Bentley responded, "Who's Krenzel?" He'd never heard of him.

Krenzel was already known, though, for his academics. He was a molecular genetics major who graduated with a GPA of 3.75. He was named the Academic All-American of the Year and won the Socrates Award as the nation's best student-athlete.

That intelligence in the classroom, which soon established Krenzel as the team's resident brainiac, carried over onto the football field, especially in 2002 when he quarterbacked Ohio State to the national championship. As head coach Jim Tressel put it, Krenzel had the "ability to comprehend and see and recognize and adjust" and "to think on his feet."

Nowhere was Krenzel's ability to "meld his academic and [his] athletic prowess" into success on the field more evident than in the Purdue game of 2002. With only 1:36 to play, the Buckeyes trailed the Boilermakers 6-3 and faced a fourth-and-one at the Purdue 37. Krenzel hit wide receiver Michael Jenkins sprinting open down the sideline for a touchdown that kept the Buckeyes' national title season on track.

The thing was -- Krenzel was using a no-huddle offense. He called that legendary play at the line of scrimmage.

While that was a really smart move Craig Krenzel pulled off against Purdue, it's a fact that we don't always follow his example. We sometimes make some pretty dumb moves.

That's because no matter how much formal education we may have, time spent in a classroom is not an accurate gauge of common sense. Folks impressed with their own smarts often grace us with erudite pronouncements that we intuitively recognize as flawed, unworkable, or simply wrong.

A good example is the observation that great intelligence and scholarship are inherently incompatible with a deep and abiding faith in God. That is, the more we know, the less we believe. Any incompatibility occurs, however, only because we begin to trust in our own wisdom rather than the wisdom of God. We forget, as Solomon did, that God is the ultimate source of all our knowledge and wisdom and that even our ability to learn is a gift from God.

Not smart at all.

I just live my life trying to make my decisions based on whether something is wrong or right.
-- Craig Krenzel on the foundation for his smart moves

Being truly smart means trusting in God's
wisdom rather than only in our own knowledge.

DAY 39

GETTING ALONG

Read Romans 14:13-23.

"For the kingdom of God is not a matter of eating and drinking, but of righteousness, peace and joy in the Holy Spirit (v. 17).

From the time his head coach moved him to quarterback, Tom Matte could rightfully say, "Woody Hayes and I hated each other for most of my career."

Hayes moved Matte in 1959 before his junior season, and Matte didn't like it one bit; he wanted to play halfback. Still, in the first of two spring games that year, he threw five touchdown passes "and ran all over the place." Any chances the two ever had of getting along as player-coach were killed for good by what Hayes did in the second game. Apparently to keep his rather rambunctious QB from getting too cocky, Hayes called the plays and then told the defense what was coming. Matte threw five interceptions.

After that, Matte decided to fumble his way back to halfback. At the one practice after the game, he pulled his hands out from under center early on purpose and fumbled six times in a row. Driven into one of his legendary temper tantrums, Hayes stormed about and screamed repeatedly, "What are we going to do?"

Finally, the frantic coach hit himself in the head so hard that, as Matte put it, "he went down like a sack of potatoes." Assistant coach Bo Schembechler told Matte, "When he wakes up, he's going to kill you."

Hayes' self-inflicted wound required five stitches to repair. He looked Matte up and told him, "You will never, ever play quarterback for me." Matte responded, "I don't want to." But Matte was the team's starting quarterback as a senior in 1960, earning both All-Big Ten and All-America honors.

Matte admitted later on that, after he graduated, his irascible coach and he "became really good friends."

The only time folks haven't disagreed among themselves was when Adam roamed the garden alone. Since then – well, we just can't seem to get along.

That includes Christians, who have never exactly been role models for peaceful coexistence among themselves. Not only does the greater body of Christ always seem to be spatting and feuding, but discord within individual churches is so commonplace that God uses church splits to grow his kingdom.

Why can't Christians get along? Perhaps it's because we take our faith so seriously, which is a good thing. But perhaps also, it's because – as Paul warned us – we can't separate the truly important from the truly trivial.

Following Christ is about achieving righteousness, joy, and peace, not about following arcane, arbitrary prescriptions for daily living or even worship. All too often we don't get along because the rules and traditions we espouse -- and not Christ's love – govern our hearts and our faith.

I had never played quarterback, and I didn't want to play quarterback.
-- Tom Matte on why he didn't get along with Woody Hayes

Christians will never get along as long as we worry about and harp on things that we shouldn't.

DAY 40

AMAZING!

Read: Luke 4:31-36.

"All the people were amazed and said to each other, 'What is this teaching? With authority and power he gives orders to evil spirits and they come out!'" (v. 36)

Cris Carter once made a catch so amazing that not even his quarterback believed the pass had been completed.

Carter, a junior, was named All-America after the 1986 season, thus becoming the first wide receiver in Ohio State history to be so honored. Despite turning pro after that season, Carter set the school record for career receptions (168). In 2000, he was named to the Ohio State Football All-Century Team.

At Ohio State, Carter "routinely made one-handed grabs that left teammates agape in practice." His most amazing catch of all, though, came in the 1985 Citrus Bowl against Brigham Young.

Quarterback Jim Karsatos recalled that during the game (won by the Buckeyes 10-7), he was chased out of the pocket and rolled to his right. As he neared the sideline, he decided to throw the ball away to avoid a sack. He spotted Carter "kind of tiptoeing the sidelines," so Karsatos figured he could sail the ball way over Carter's head to avoid a penalty for intentional grounding. "So I wind it up and let it go high and outside," Karsatos recalled, just before a Brigham Young defender knocked him out of bounds.

As he picked himself up, Karsatos was surprised to find the defender both glaring at him and cursing at him. "I can't believe you completed that pass with me knocking you down like that," he said. "I threw that ball away," Karsatos replied. "No, you didn't. He caught it," the hacked-off defender snapped.

Karsatos still didn't believe it. Only when he saw the amazing catch on film did he appreciate what had happened. Carter snared the ball left-handed "at least a yard out of bounds," Karsatos described. Then to get his feet in bounds, "I swear to this day that he actually levitated."

The word amazing defines the limits of what you believe to be plausible or usual. The Grand Canyon, the birth of your children, those last-second Buckeye wins -- they're amazing! You've never seen anything like that before!

Some people in Galilee felt the same way when they encountered Jesus. Jesus amazed them with the authority of his teaching, and he wowed them with his power over spirit beings. People everywhere just couldn't quit talking about him.

It would have been amazing had they not been amazed. They were, after all, witnesses to the most amazing spectacle in the history of the world: God himself was right there among them walking, talking, teaching, preaching, and healing.

Their amazement should be a part of your life too because Jesus still lives. The almighty God of the universe seeks to spend time with you every day – because he loves you. Amazing!

When I saw it on film, it just blew me away.
-- Jim Karsatos on Cris Carter's amazing catch vs. BYU

Everything about God is amazing,
but perhaps most amazing of all is that
he loves us and desires our company.

OHIO STATE

DAY 41

THE GOOD FIGHT

Read 1 Corinthians 10:1-6.

"Though we live in the world, we do not wage war as the world does. The weapons we fight with are not the weapons of the world" (vv. 3-4a).

Ohio State's basketball team was once viciously attacked during a game in "one of the ugliest scenes in the history of sports."

On Jan. 25, 1972, the Buckeyes met Minnesota in Minneapolis in a battle of Big Ten undefeateds. Minnesota led 32-30 with 11:41 to play, but Ohio State scored ten straight points and took control of the game. As the clock ran down and defeat was inevitable, the crowd turned ugly, throwing debris onto the floor.

With 36 seconds to play and Ohio State ahead 50-44, the thin veneer of civility dissipated when seven-foot Buckeye center Luke Witte drove for what promised to be the game-clinching layup. A Minnesota player fouled him hard and followed up by hitting him in the face with an overhand right hook. Before Witte could get up, the Minnesota player kneed him in the groin.

The arena immediately "erupted in a swirl of flying fists." Ohio State guard Dave Merchant was pummeled with a barrage of punches. One Minnesota player rushed off the bench "to where Witte was lying helpless and viciously stomped [his] neck and face." Another player jumped on top of Buckeye sub Mark Wagar, wrestled him to the floor, and punched him repeatedly.

Then the fans rioted, rushing onto the floor and attacking the

OSU players. "For a scary, improbable interval of one minute and 35 seconds, they came swinging and kicking at the Buckeyes from all sides of the floor." When order was restored, Minnesota's athletic director declared the game to be over.

Three Ohio State players were taken to the hospital. The victim of what Ohio's governor described as "a public mugging," Witte, who became a minister, spent time in intensive care and needed 29 stitches to repair the damage. Gopher fans had booed him "as he was helped, bleeding and semiconscious, from the floor."

Violence is not the Christian way, but what about confrontation? Following Jesus' admonition to turn the other cheek has rendered many a Christian meek and mild in the name of obedience. But we need to remember that the Lord we follow once bullwhipped a bunch of folks who turned God's temple into a flea market.

With Christianity in America under attack as never before, we must stand up for and fight for our faith. Who else is there to stand up for Jesus if not you? Our pretty little planet -- including our nation -- is a battleground between good and evil. We are far from helpless in this fight because God has provided us with a powerful set of weapons. Prayer, faith, hope, love, the Word of God itself and the Holy Spirit -- these are the weapons at our command with which to vanquish evil and godlessness.

We are called by God to use them, to fight the good fight, not just in our own lives but in our nation and in our world.

It was an ugly, cowardly display of violence.
-- SI writer William F. Reed on the Minnesota attack of '72

'Stand Up, Stand Up for Jesus' is not an antiquated hymn but a contemporary call to battle for God.

DAY 42

HEAD GAMES

Read Job 28.

"The fear of the Lord -- that is wisdom, and to shun evil is understanding" (v. 28).

Francis Aloysius Schmidt was quite correctly labeled an "offensive genius." Using his head to create and diagram football plays did not, however, keep him from being absent-minded.

Schmidt was hired away from TCU in the spring of 1934 to coach the Buckeyes, and he led them to a 39-16-1 record over seven seasons. Though Schmidt was unknown in Columbus, his genius at creating a wide-open offense quickly won Ohio State fans over.

He was an innovator, the first Ohio State coach to use the I-formation. He dreamed up plays that employed reverses, double reverses, and laterals out of any formation, even teaching his players not to hesitate to make a risky pitch to a teammate if they were about to be tackled. He had his quarterbacks paste or draw plays inside their helmets so they could remember the offense.

Schmidt is responsible for one of the great cliches in sports and one of the greatest of Buckeye traditions. Asked once about Michigan, he replied, "They put their pants on one leg at a time just like everybody else." That remark led to the formation of the Michigan Pants Club and the awarding of the Gold Pants charm to each player or coach who beat the Wolverines.

Schmidt was constantly diagramming plays and formations using notebooks, tablecloths, or whatever he had on hand. He

BUCKEYES

once was so caught up in thinking up new plays that he forgot where he was at the time: seated in his car, which was on a jack at a Columbus filling station having its oil changed. A new play finished to his satisfaction, his note pad held in front of him as he reviewed his creation, he opened his car door and stepped out. Tradition differs as to whether he fell all eight feet to the ground or whether station attendants managed to get to Schmidt in time to save the absent-minded head coach from serious injury.

You're a thinking person. When you talk about using your head, you're speaking of having logic and reason as part of your psyche. A coach's bad call frustrates you and your children's inexplicable behavior flummoxes you. Why can't people just think things through?

That goes for matters of faith too. Jesus doesn't tell you to turn your brain off when you walk into a church or open the Bible. In fact, when you seek Jesus, you seek him heart, soul, body, and mind. The mind of the master should be the master of your mind so that you consider every situation in your life through the critical lens of the mind of Christ. With your head and your heart, you encounter God, who is, after all, the true source of wisdom.

To know Jesus is not to stop thinking; it is to start thinking divinely.

Football is more mental than physical, no matter how it looks from the stands.

-- Pro Hall-of-Fame linebacker Ray Nitschke

**Since God is the source of all wisdom,
it's only logical that you encounter him
with your mind as well as your emotions.**

DAY 43

FOOD FOR THOUGHT

Read Genesis 9:1-7.

"Everything that lives and moves will be food for you. Just as I gave you the green plants, I now give you everything" *(v. 3).*

Jelly and an attack watermelon figure in Buckeye lore.

Punter Tom Skladany (1973-76) was a three-time All-America who didn't particularly like cold weather. During cold-weather practices, he sometimes led the punters and kickers into the locker room for "eating jelly doughnuts, drinking hot chocolate, playing cards, and sometimes even studying."

One time, though, the trainer came in and bellowed out that coach Woody Hayes wanted him. "I went out there running as fast as I could," Skladany recalled. The players burst out laughing when they saw him; he had jelly from a doughnut all over his face. "I stayed outside after that," Skladany said.

Offensive lineman Barney Renard (1973-76) once joined a few of his fellow Buckeyes in a late-night raid of their dorm's cafeteria. To their great delight, they found a whole watermelon in a refrigerator and snitched it.

Back in their room high up on their dorm, though, they discovered they didn't have a knife to cut the melon with. One of them suggested they throw the melon out a window. "So," Renard said, "two of us chuck this big watermelon out the window" and leaned out to watch it fall. To their horror, they realized the melon

BUCKEYES

was headed right toward Hayes' parked El Camino.

Their horror turned to relief when the melon missed the car, landing right next to it and exploding, in the process "splattering watermelon seeds, juice, and part of that watermelon all down the side of Woody's El Camino."

That adventure squelched the group's appetite for the night. Renard said, "There was a little stir the next day about it, but [Hayes] never found out who did it."

Belly up to the buffet, boys and girls, for barbecue, sirloin steak, grilled chicken, and fried catfish with hush puppies and cheese grits. Rachael Ray's a household name; hamburger joints, pizza parlors, and taco stands lurk on every corner; and we have television channels devoted exclusively to food. We love our chow.

Food is one of God's really good ideas, but consider the complex divine plan that begins with a seed and ends with corn-on-the-cob. The creator of all life devised a system in which living things are sustained and nourished physically through the sacrifice of other living things in a way similar to what Christ underwent to save us spiritually. Whether it's fast food or home-cooked, every-thing we eat is a gift from God secured through a divine plan in which some plants and animals have given up their lives.

Pausing to give thanks before we dive in seems the least we can do.

I cut down to six meals a day.

-- Charles Barkley on losing weight

**God created a system that nourishes us
through the sacrifice of other living things;
that's worth a thank-you.**

MAKING IT RIGHT

Read Exodus 22:1-15.

"A thief must certainly make restitution" (v. 2b).

Howard "Hopalong" Cassady once had his Heisman Trophy stolen but subsequently recovered it when the thieves dumped it into the garbage.

The running back/defensive back Woody Hayes called "the most inspirational player I have ever seen" scored three touchdowns in his first varsity game in 1952 and in the process earned a lifelong nickname. Sportswriters said he "hopped all over the field like the performing cowboy," a reference to the fictional character Hopalong Cassady. In his four seasons, Cassady scored 37 touchdowns in 36 games and never had a pass completed on him. He was All-America in 1954 and '55 and won the Heisman Trophy in 1955 by the widest margin ever to that time.

Perhaps the only time Cassady had any issues at State came in 1953 when he was having problems executing an off-tackle run at practice. Hayes brought in backup Robert Croce, who ran the play perfectly, bursting through the line for more than twenty yards. Hayes pointed out the problem to his star: "Croce was just slow enough to hit the hole. You're hitting the line too fast!"

Cassady went on to play eight seasons of pro football with the Detroit Lions. A star shortstop at Ohio State, he worked for more than thirty years as a scout for the New York Yankees. In the mid-1980s while Cassady was on a scouting trip, some thieves burglarized his home and stole a number of awards, including the Heisman Trophy. They kept the sterling-silver plaques and trophies but discarded the bronze Heisman Trophy in a garbage can where a sanitation worker found it and called school officials. Several of the trophy's fingers were broken, but the Heisman was repaired and returned to its owner.

Buckle up your seat belt. Wear a bicycle or motorcycle helmet. Use your pooper scooper to clean up after your dog. Don't even think about littering. Picky ordinances, picky laws – in all their great abundance, they're an inescapable part of our modern lives.

When Moses came stumbling down Mt. Sinai after spending time as God's secretary, he brought with him a whole mess of laws and regulations, many of which undoubtedly seem picky to us today. What some of them provide, though, are practical examples of what for God is the basic principle underlying the theft of personal property: what is wrong must be made right.

While most of us today won't have to worry too much about the theft of livestock such as oxen, sheep, and donkeys (or of Heisman trophies), making what is wrong right remains a way of life for Christians. To get right with other people requires anything from restitution to apologies. To get right with God requires Jesus Christ.

The price of silver was way up and they just didn't realize the value of the Heisman.
-- Howard Cassady on the thieves who stole his Heisman Trophy

To make right the wrong of stealing requires restitution; to make right our relationship with God requires Jesus Christ.

DAY 45

A GOOD IMPRESSION

Read John 1:1-18.

"In the beginning was the Word, and the Word was with God, and the Word was God. . . . The Word became flesh and made his dwelling among us" (vv. 1, 14).

Sam Marder had only one chance to make a good impression on Ohio State's Linda Kalafatis. The head softball coach didn't see too much.

Marder was in high school in California when she e-mailed Kalafatis about playing softball for the Buckeyes. She wasn't being heavily recruited by the state schools, and Ohio State intrigued her because her grandfather had graduated from there.

Kalafatis followed up by asking other coaches about Marder. They pretty much all told her that the senior catcher was a decent hitter. That was enough to spur Kalafatis into taking the long plane ride to California to watch Marder play.

She didn't get much of a chance. In her second at-bat, Marder was hit by a pitch that broke her hand. Still, the trip wasn't a waste of time. Kalafatis had arrived early enough to watch Marder take batting practice. And in her first at-bat in the game, Marder ripped a line drive off the center-field wall. It wasn't much, but it was enough. Kalafatis offered her a scholarship.

What Kalafatis got out of that quick impression was arguably the greatest softball player Ohio State has ever had. From 2007-2010, Marder was a three-time All-America, the first one in school history, and was four times All-Big Ten. In 2010, she was the Ohio State Female Athlete of the Year. She was the leader of a senior class that won 159 games and advanced to the program's first-ever super-regional (in 2009). She set Buckeye career records for home runs (61), RBIs (191), and walks.

Marder made quite an impression of her own once she arrived in Columbus. She hit seven home runs in her first 48 at bats as a freshman.

That guy in the apartment next door. A job search complete with interview. A twenty-year class reunion. The new neighbors. We are constantly about the fraught task of wanting to make an impression on people. We want them to remember us, obviously in a flattering way.

We make that impression, good or bad, generally in two ways. Even with instant communication on the Internet – perhaps especially with the Internet – we primarily influence the opinion others have of us by our words. After that, we can advance to the next level by making an impression with our actions.

God gave us an impression of himself in exactly the same way. In Jesus, God took the unprecedented step of appearing to mortals as one of us, as mere flesh and bone. We now know for all time the sorts of things God does and the sorts of things God says. In Jesus, God put his divine foot forward to make a good impression on each one of us.

It's a good thing we got there early enough to watch her warm up.
-- Linda Kalafatis on her trip to California to see Sam Marder

Through Jesus' words and actions,
God seeks to impress us with his love.

THE MOTHER LODE

Read John 19:25-30.

"Near the cross of Jesus stood his mother" (v. 25).

Eddie George was crying, but he had good reason: His mother was sending him away.

Eddie was 15 years old when his mother, Donna, made the heartrending but crucial decision to send her son away from his hometown of Philadelphia to enroll at Fork Union Military Academy in Virginia. She had her reasons. All Eddie wanted to do was play football. "He hated school, and his grades, always poor, were only getting worse." "This is what you need. This is what you're going to get," she said, sticking by her guns through her son's whining and his tears. They both cried the day he left.

Fort Union was a strict place, instilling the discipline young Eddie needed. The school also had a football team with even more rules to follow. Eddie took some convincing, but he caught on. "His size and strength grew, and his defiant attitude toward authority figures softened."

In 1992, George came to Columbus. He saw little action his first two seasons, but his junior year he was the featured tailback. Then came his mammoth senior season in 1995 when he rushed for 1,927 yards and led the nation in scoring. He set a school record for pass receptions by a running back. In the 41-3 win over Illinois that season, he set a school record by rushing for 314 yards, breaking the previous record of 274 set by Keith Byars.

In December, George achieved the pinnacle of college football success when he was named OSU's fifth winner of the Heisman Trophy. He dropped his head into his hands, his mind flashing back to the day his mother "had shipped him off . . . against his will but for the betterment of his development as a young man and a football player."

He rose and hugged the other finalists and Ohio State head coach John Cooper. He saved his last hug for his mother.

Mamas often do that sort of thing Donna George did for Eddie: sacrifice her personal happiness for the sake of her child. No mother in history, though, has faced a challenge to match that of Mary, whom God chose to be the mother of Jesus. Like mamas and their children throughout time, Mary experienced both joy and perplexity in her relationship with her son.

To the end, though, Mary stood by her boy. She followed him all the way to his execution, an act of love and bravery since Jesus was condemned as an enemy of the Roman Empire.

But just as mothers like Mary and Donna George – and perhaps yours -- would apparently do anything for their children, so will God do anything out of love for his children. After all, that was God on the cross at the foot of which Mary stood, and he was dying for you, one of his children.

I was hardheaded, and I didn't listen. Before it got worse, my mom had to send me away.
— *Eddie George*

Mamas often sacrifice for their children, but God, too, will do anything out of love for his children, including dying on a cross.

DAY 47

DIVIDED LOYALTIES

Read Matthew 6:1-24.

"No one can serve two masters" (v. 24a).

Former Buckeye football players are usually among the school's most loyal alums. But what about when you play football both for *and* against Ohio State? At least three Buckeyes did just that.

During World War II, Ohio State's football team played some non-collegiate teams. The 1942 national champs began the season by whipping Fort Knox 59-0 and ended it by beating the Iowa Seahawks, a team from the U.S. Navy Pre-Flight School, 41-12. Ohio State also played a pair of games against military teams in 1943 and one in 1944. Those circumstances led to an unusual situation for a pair of Buckeye players.

Charlie Ream was an end for the Buckeyes who lettered three times (1935-37). Five years after he graduated, he played against OSU as a member of that Iowa Seahawks team. "The strangest thing happened to me," he said in referring to the circumstances that led to his lining up against his alma mater. "Still, it was a thrill to go back to Columbus to play them," he said. Nevertheless, he was refused admittance to the OSU locker room.

Fullback James Langhurst was also part of that Iowa Pre-Flight team. He was the MVP of the 1938 OSU team, leading the Big Ten in scoring, and was captain of the 1940 squad as a senior. He rushed for 108 yards against his alma mater in that 1942 game.

Perhaps the most bizarre instance of divided loyalties, though, involved John T. (J.T.) White, an end for the national champions of 1942. "I still cherish the pair of gold pants we received for beating Michigan," he said decades later. He spent three years in the military during World War II and went back to school on the GI Bill when the war ended.

What made his situation strange, though, is that White went to Michigan and started at center for the '47 Wolverines that won the national title. "I am sure that no other player has ever played for two universities who were national champions," he once said.

You probably understand the stress that comes with divided loyalties. The Christian work ethic drives you to be successful. The world, however, often makes demands and presents images that conflict with your devotion to God: movies deride God; couples play musical beds in TV sitcoms; and TV dramas portray Christians as killers following God's orders.

It's Sunday morning and the office will be quiet or the golf course won't be crowded. What do you do when your heart and loyalties are pulled in two directions? Jesus knew of the struggle we face; that's why he spoke of not being able to serve "two masters," that we wind up serving one and despising the other. Put in terms of either serving God or despising God, the choice is stark and clear.

Your loyalty is to God -- always.

Here I was, playing my alma mater -- that was awful strange to me.
-- Charlie Ream on playing for the Iowa Seahawks in 1942

God does not condemn you for being successful
and enjoying popular culture, but your loyalty
must lie first and foremost with him.

DAY 48

FAIL-SAFE

Read Luke 22:54-62.

"Peter remembered the word the Lord had spoken to him: 'Before the rooster crows today, you will disown me three times.' And he went outside and wept bitterly" (vv. 61b-62).

Failure as a pro led Devin Barclay to success as an amateur.

Barclay was so good in high school that he signed a professional soccer contract in 2001 when he was 17. His career didn't go the way he hoped, however. His team folded after his rookie year, and he spent four injury-plagued seasons as a journeyman. He played in only nineteen games during those four seasons and didn't score a goal.

His last team was the Columbus Crew, and he stayed in town after he left pro soccer. He realized he would need a college education to compete in the real world and started at Ohio State in 2006. He began thinking about kicking for the football team but had a slight problem: He had never kicked a football before.

But Barclay met the owner of Easy Living Deli, Vlade Janakievski, who had set multiple kicking records for the Buckeyes from 1977-80 and had also played on the soccer team. He agreed to help Barclay learn to kick a football. "As soon as I took him out, I could tell he had that touch and I knew he could kick," Janakievski said.

Barclay made the team as a walk-on in the spring of 2008, but he sat behind Ryan Pretorius and Aaron Pettrey and didn't play at all during the season. An injury to Pettrey in 2009 promoted him to the top spot. His 39-yard field goal in overtime against Iowa sent the Buckeyes to the Rose Bowl. With one play, Barclay was propelled "from complete obscurity into Buckeye lore."

In 2010, as a 27-year-old senior, Barclay was the oldest player on a major college team. He was also one of the most accurate kickers in the country. He led the team in scoring with 122 points on 20 of 24 field goals and 62 extra points without a miss.

As it was with Devin Barclay's pro soccer career, failure is usually defined by expectations. A baseball player who hits .300 is a star, but he fails seventy percent of the time. We grumble about a postal system that manages to deliver billions of items without a hitch.

And we are often our own harshest critics, beating ourselves up for our failings because we expected better. Never mind that our expectations were unrealistic to begin with.

The bad news about life is that failure – unlike success -- is inevitable. Only one man walked this earth perfectly and we're not him. The good news about life, however, is that failure isn't permanent. In life, we always have time to reverse our failures as did Peter, he who failed our Lord so abjectly.

The same cannot be said of death. In death we eternally suffer the consequences of our failure to follow that one perfect man.

It just helped me grow up and learn what works and how to find the patterns of success.
-- Devin Barclay on his failed pro soccer career

Only one failure in life dooms us to eternal failure in death: failing to follow Jesus Christ.

DAY 49

PRECIOUS MEMORIES

Read 1 Thessalonians 3:6-13.

"Timothy . . . has brought good news about your faith and love. He has told us that you always have pleasant memories of us" (v. 6).

Tributes are usually reserved for legendary players who set all kinds of records, but the OSU men's soccer program remembers a freshman who played only a handful of matches.

Freshman Connor Senn walked on to the Buckeye soccer team in the fall of 2001 and made the starting lineup right away. Senn played with a passion for the game and was "hyper-competitive while still being a down-to-earth and happy-go-lucky person."

On Sept. 26, in Akron during the eighth match of the season, Senn slumped to the ground. "I was at the other end of the field, but I could tell from the panic around him that it might be bad," said his father, Lance, who played tennis for the Buckeyes in the 1970s. It was as bad as the father could imagine. His 18-year-old son died, the victim of an undetectable heart abnormality.

The shattered Buckeye team rallied around the mantra "Play like Connor today" for the rest of the season. It remains a source of inspiration today, just one aspect of the program's insistence that Senn be remembered. "Right from the start, even before kids commit to us, they've already heard the story about Connor," said coach John Bluem. A tree has been planted in Senn's honor; a plaque in the stadium remembers him; each spring the program plays the Conner Senn Memorial match that raises money for a scholarship in Senn's name.

Connor Senn not only is remembered but continues to inspire Buckeye soccer players today.

While you probably don't enjoy dwelling on such things, your whole life -- like Connor Senn's -- will one day be only a memory. With that knowledge in hand, you can control much about your inevitable funeral. You can, for instance, select a funeral home, purchase a cemetery plot, pick out your casket or a tasteful urn, designate those who will deliver your eulogy, and make other less important decisions about your send-off.

What you cannot control about your death, however, is how you will be remembered and whether your demise leaves a gaping hole in the lives of those with whom you shared your life or a pothole that's quickly paved over. What determines whether those nice words someone will say about you are heartfelt truth or pleasant fabrications? What determines whether the tears that fall at your death result from heartfelt grief or a sinus infection?

Love does. Just as Paul wrote, the love you give away during your life decides whether or not memories of you will be precious and pleasant.

I think he'd be happy. Probably he is happy, looking down on us and seeing what we're doing to carry on his memory and his tradition.
— *Coach John Bluem on Connor Senn*

How you will be remembered after you die is largely determined by how much and how deeply you love others now.

DAY 50

LESSON LEARNED

Read Psalm 143.

"Teach me to do your will, for you are my God" (v. 10).

One scary night was all it took for Rex Kern to learn a vital lesson about riding with Woody Hayes.

Writer Jeff Snook said, "Perhaps no player was ever closer to Woody Hayes than Rex Kern (1968-70), the quarterback of his last national championship team. He was one of Woody's all-time favorites, if not his favorite." Offensive tackle Dave Cheney, who roomed with Kern for two years, agreed, recalling, "We always teased Rex about Woody being his father."

It came as no surprise, therefore, when Hayes asked the freshman quarterback to ride with him on a recruiting trip one winter evening. As Kern remembered the night, "It was snowing like crazy," and as they rode Hayes was talking football "and not paying attention to the road. We can't see 10 feet in front of us, and he is going 60 or 65 miles per hour."

Sure enough, the car hit a slick spot and hydroplaned. "We do a complete 360 on this small country road," Kern said. "We ended up in the same direction we were heading, and he just keeps driving." Neither one of them said a word until a few minutes later when Hayes said. "You don't tell anybody that just happened, especially my wife, Anne!"

Kern did remain mum, but he needed a little reminding from Hayes. At their destination, somebody said, "Coach, I didn't

BUCKEYES

think you would make it tonight." Kern piped up, "I didn't think we would make it either!" That's when his arm received a hearty squeeze from the coach, a reminder to keep quiet.

Back at Columbus, Kern did tell assistant coach Tiger Ellison about the incident. The coach said, "Rex, one thing you've got to learn. If you go with Woody, you have to be the driver! Nobody lets Woody drive them!"

As Rex Kern's harrowing trip with Woody Hayes illustrates, learning about anything in life requires a combination of education and experience. Education is the accumulation of facts that we call knowledge; experience is the acquisition of wisdom and discernment, which add depth to our knowledge in the form of purpose and understanding.

The most difficult way to learn is trial and error: dive in blindly and mess up. The best way to learn is through example coupled with a set of instructions: Someone has gone ahead to show you the way and has written down all the information you need to follow.

In teaching us the way to live godly lives, God chose the latter method. He set down in his book the habits, actions, and attitudes that make for a way of life in accordance with his wishes. He also sent us Jesus to explain and to illustrate.

God teaches us not only how to exist but how to live. We just need to be attentive students.

It's what you learn after you know it all that counts.
— John Wooden

To learn from Jesus is to learn what life is all about and how God means for us to live it.

DAY 51

TEN TO REMEMBER

Read Exodus 20:1-17.

"God spoke all these words: 'I am the Lord your God . . . .
You shall have no other gods before me'" (vv. 1, 3).

In 1996, the Buckeyes embarrassed Pittsburgh 72-0, the biggest blowout in the modern era. But there have been enough laughers to assemble a convincing list of the top ten beatdowns since 1950.

The Ohio State University beat Indiana 56-0 in 1957 and Wisconsin 56-0 in 1975, the games with the tenth biggest margin of defeat in modern OSU history. The ninth biggest was a 64-6 blowout of Utah in 1986; in that game, the Buckeyes set a school record that still stands with 715 yards of offense.

Wisconsin makes the list again, coming in at No. 8 by losing 59-0 in 1979. The seventh biggest slaughter in Buckeye football history is 1973's 60-0 romp over Northwestern. The Buckeyes scored all eight touchdowns in less than a quarter and a half.

Numbers 6 and 5 on the list of State's most overwhelming wins are two 62-point defeats: 62-0 over TCU in 1969 and 83-21 over Iowa in 1950. In the Iowa game, Heisman-Trophy winner Vic Janowicz accounted for six touchdowns (one rushing, four passing, and one punt return) and kicked ten PATs. The 83 points hung on the Hawkeyes is the most in modern times.

Tied for fourth and third among OSU runaways are the 70-7 whipping of Rice in 1996 and the 63-0 defeat of Northwestern in 1980. No. 2 on the list is the 70-6 embarrassment of Northwestern only a year later in 1981. And then comes the 72-point slaughter of Pitt that tops the list. OSU scored on its first ten possessions and led 52-0 at halftime.

That runaway still sits way behind the greatest blowout in OSU gridiron history, the 128-0 pasting laid on Oberlin College in 1916 by the school's first Big-Ten champions.

For OSU fans, these ten modern blowouts (and one from the dawn of the program) are indeed games to remember for the ages.

You've got your list and you're ready to go: a gallon of paint and a water hose from the hardware store; chips, peanuts, and sodas from the grocery store for watching tonight's football game with your buddies; the tickets for the band concert. Your list helps you remember.

God also made a list once of things he wanted you to remember; it's called the Ten Commandments. Just as your list reminds you to do something, so does God's list remind you of how you are to act in your dealings with other people and with him.

A life dedicated to Jesus is a life devoted to relationships, and God's list emphasizes that the social life and the spiritual life of the faithful cannot be sundered. God's relationship to you is one of unceasing, unqualified love, and you are to mirror that divine love in your relationships with others. In case you forget, you have a list.

Society today treats the Ten Commandments as if they were the ten suggestions. Never compromise on right or wrong.
-- College baseball coach Gordie Gillespie

God's list is a set of instructions on how you are to conduct yourself with other people and with him.

![OHIO STATE]

DAY 52

JUST PERFECT

Read Matthew 5:43-48.

"Be perfect, therefore, as your heavenly Father is perfect"
(v. 48).

What's the perfect ending to a perfect Buckeye season? Beating Michigan.

"Let's face it: The only reason [Jim] Tressel has a job in Columbus is that his predecessor had won two games in 13 tries against the Wolverines." So wrote *Sports Illustrated*'s Austin Murphy shortly after Tressel was hired. When the Buckeyes hosted Michigan on Nov. 23, 2002, they were seeking Tressel's second straight win in the game that each year made or ruined the season. On this day, a win would cap a perfect 13-0 season and propel Ohio State into the game for the national championship in the Fiesta Bowl.

Tressel had his players take a low-key approach to the biggest football game of their lives, so they would remain poised under pressure. They did just that. Trailing 9-7 in the fourth quarter, the Buckeyes marched for the game-winning touchdown and then shut down Michigan's last-ditch efforts to save itself.

The final period was ticking away when Tressel called a play-action pass inserted especially for this game. Freshman tailback Maurice Clarett slid to the left sideline, and quarterback Craig Krenzel hit him with a perfect strike. The 26-yard play gave OSU a first down at the Michigan six. Two plays later tailback Maurice Hall scored on a perfectly executed option play with 4:55 left in

the game. The final of 14-9 was on the scoreboard.

The defense had to pull off a pair of plays to wrap up the perfect regular season. From the Buckeye 30, junior defensive end Darrion Scott sacked the Wolverine quarterback and forced a fumble that Will Smith recovered with 2:02 left. On the game's last play, safety Will Allen hauled down an interception.

Just perfect.

Nobody's perfect; we all make mistakes every day. We botch our personal relationships; at work we seek competence and not perfection. To insist upon personal or professional perfection in our lives is to establish an impossibly high standard that will eventually destroy us physically, emotionally, and mentally.

Yet that is exactly the standard God sets for us. Our love is to be perfect, never ceasing, never failing, never qualified – just the way God loves us. And Jesus didn't limit his command to goody-two-shoes types and preachers. All of his disciples are to be perfect as they navigate their way through the world's ambiguous definition and understanding of love.

But that's impossible! Well, not necessarily, if to love perfectly is to serve God wholeheartedly and to follow Jesus with single-minded devotion. Anyhow, in his perfect love for us, God makes allowance for our imperfect love and the consequences of it in the perfection of Jesus.

If we chase perfection, we can catch excellence.

-- *Vince Lombardi*

In his perfect love for us, God provides a way
for us to escape the consequences
of our imperfect love for him: Jesus.

DAY 53

RESPECTFULLY YOURS

Read Mark 8:31-38.

"He then began to teach them that the Son of Man must suffer many things and be rejected by the elders, chief priests and teachers of the law, and that he must be killed" (v. 31).

The Badgers learned a pointed lesson: When you don't give the Buckeyes the respect they deserve, you pay for it.

On Feb. 12, 2011, Ohio State, undefeated and ranked No. 1 in the country, had a 15-point lead against 13th-ranked Wisconsin, but was outscored 30-8 over the next nine minutes and lost. After the game, national freshman-of-the-year Jared Sullinger said a Badger fan spit in his face. The Wisconsin head coach was only slightly less rude, declaring, "We won the game. Deal with it."

The Badgers came to Columbus on March 6, and the Buckeyes didn't forget. Before the game, officials distributed 1,400 scarlet towels to a packed house; they read "Deal With It" in white letters. When the monitors over midcourt flashed a picture of the Badger coach before the game, the crowd responded with very loud and hearty boos and catcalls.

"Deal with it" was to be the chant from the crowd as the game wore on. The once-disrespected Buckeyes did indeed deal with it. They simply slaughtered the 10th-ranked Badgers.

Wisconsin actually stayed reasonably close for a good part of the game. The Badgers trailed only 56-45 with 14:15 left. After

that, though, the Buckeyes put on a show that made sure they didn't have to worry about respect anymore.

Senior guard Jon Diebler, who scored 27 points and hit 7 of 8 three-point shots, led a 10-0 run that blew the game open. "The rest of the game was a matter of killing time until the Buckeyes could cut down the nets and raise the Big Ten trophy."

When the carnage was over, Ohio State had set a pair of NCAA records by hitting 14 straight threes and 14 of 15 for the game. The Buckeyes had gained some respect with a 93-65 romp.

Rodney Dangerfield made a good living as a comedian with a repertoire that was basically only countless variations on one punch line: "I don't get no respect." Dangerfield was successful because he struck a chord with his audience. No one wants to play football for a program that no one respects. You want the respect, the esteem, and the regard that you feel you've earned.

But more often than not, you don't get it. Still, you shouldn't feel too badly; you're in good company. In the ultimate example of disrespect, Jesus – the very Son of God -- was treated as the worst type of criminal. He was arrested, bound, scorned, ridiculed, spit upon, tortured, condemned, and executed.

God allowed his son to undergo such treatment because of his high regard and his love for you. You are respected by almighty God! Could anyone else's respect really matter?

You don't have to like me; just respect me.

-- Woody Hayes

**You may not get the respect you deserve,
but at least nobody's spitting on you
and driving nails into you as they did to Jesus.**

DAY 54

REVELATION

Read Isaiah 53.

"But he was pierced for our transgressions, he was crushed for our iniquities; the punishment that brought us peace was upon him, and by his wounds we are healed" (v. 5).

When freshman running back Brandon Saine scored on the last play of the game, he turned strength coach Eric Lichter into an unlikely prophet.

The 10th-ranked Buckeyes of 2007 hit the road to take on the undefeated Washington Huskies. They would finish the regular season 11-1 and in the BCS championship game, but on Sept. 15, they were seeking vindication for their high ranking.

They didn't earn it the first half, trailing 7-3 after the Huskies scored with three seconds on the clock. In a halftime speech, Lichter told the Buckeyes "a really sweet team would . . . hang 30 on the Huskies in the second half." That struck right tackle Kirk Barton as a rather strange prediction. "I was like, 'How are we going to score 30?'" he said, doing the math. "Why not 28 or 35?"

In only 39 dynamic seconds in the third quarter, the Buckeyes turned the game completely around. "They were stumbling, and we were just going and going and going," said left tackle Alex Boone about the 39 seconds.

All that fun in the quarter started with 9:36 on the clock when quarterback Todd Boeckman checked off at the line and found

Brian Robiskie with a 68-yard bomb and a 10-7 OSU lead. After Washington fumbled the kickoff and freshman cornerback James Scott recovered the ball, Beanie Wells scored from 14 yards out with 8:57 in the third. 39 seconds, 14 points, and a 17-7 lead.

The Buckeyes led 27-14 when Saine raced in for a 37-yard TD on the game's final play. That meant no extra point try -- which also meant the Buckeyes had scored an unlikely 30 points in the last half. Just as Eric Lichter had predicted.

In our jaded age, we have pretty much relegated prophecy to dark rooms in which mysterious women peer into crystal balls or clasp our sweaty palms while uttering some vague generalities. At best, we understand a prophet as someone who predicts future events as Eric Lichter did.

Within the pages of the Bible, though, we encounter something radically different. A prophet is a messenger from God, one who relays divine revelation to others.

Prophets seem somewhat foreign to us because in one very real sense the age of prophecy is over. In the name of Jesus, we have access to God through our prayers and through scripture. In searching for God's will for our lives, we seek divine revelation.

We may speak only for ourselves and not for the greater body of Christ, but we do not need a prophet to discern what God would have us do. We need faith in the one whose birth, life, and death fulfilled more than 300 Bible prophecies.

It was pretty funny how it worked out.
-- Kirk Barton on scoring 30 points in the last half vs. Washington

Persons of faith continuously seek a word
from God for their lives.

DAY 55

CHOICES

Read Deuteronomy 30:15-20.

"I have set before you life and death, blessings and curses. Now choose life, so that you and your children may live" (v. 19).

Two-time All-American Warren Amling once made such a bad choice at a coin toss that the Buckeyes lost every option they had.

Amling was a Buckeye All-America at guard in 1945 and at tackle in 1946. He is a member of both the OSU Athletic Hall of Fame and the National Football Foundation Hall of Fame.

Despite his obvious ability, Amling wasn't recruited out of high school, and no one at Ohio State asked him to walk on. His roommate his freshman season was legendary kicker and tackle Lou Groza, who encouraged Amling to join him at practice. As Amling put it, he "eventually worked [his] way onto the team."

He called the play in the 1944 Michigan game that resulted in the decisive touchdown in the 18-14 win that concluded an undefeated season. Amling thought that with the win the Big Ten champions were also national champs, but "Army, because of the war, was voted number one. I think we were the civilian champs."

Head coach Carroll Widdoes appointed Amling the team's acting captain for the Illinois game of 1945 (which the Buckeyes won 27-2). The coach gave his captain explicit instructions as to what he was to do: "If we win the toss, defend the north goal, since the wind is blowing from the north. If we lose the toss and

the Illini take the north goal, we will receive."

But, as Amling pointed out, "Then, as now, the wind in the stadium played tricks." Just before the toss, he glanced at the flag and saw that the wind had changed directions. When he won the toss, Amling followed his coach's instructions and took the wind, opting to defend the south goal. Illinois chose to receive. As Amling jogged off the field, he glanced at the flag and discovered to his dismay that the wind had changed directions again.

Widdoes asked him, "What did we get?"

Amling correctly and succinctly replied, "Neither."

Your life is the sum of the choices you've made. That is, you have arrived at this moment and this place in your life because of the choices you made in your past. Your love of the Buckeyes. Your spouse or the absence of one. Mechanic, teacher, or beautician. Condo in downtown Cincinnati or ranch home in Lima. Dog, cat, or goldfish. You chose; you live with the results.

That includes the most important choice you will ever have to make: faith or the lack of it. That we have the ability to make decisions when faced with alternatives is a gift from God, who allows that faculty even when he's part of the choice. We can choose whether or not we will love him. God reminds us, though, that this particular choice has extreme consequences: Choosing God's way is life; choosing against him is death.

Life or death. What choice is that?

Thank goodness, Coach was an understanding man.
-- Warren Amling on the coin toss against Illinois

God gives you the freedom to choose:
life or death; what kind of choice is that?

STORY TIME

Read Luke 8:26-39.

"'Return home and tell how much God has done for you.'
So the man went away and told all over town how much
Jesus had done for him" (v. 39).

Stories about gasoline and a freshman's tie attest to how deeply Woody Hayes disliked not just the University of Michigan but the whole state.

In 1972, Hayes and assistant coach Ed Ferkany were driving home in a rental car one evening after a recruiting trip to Detroit. Ferkany noticed the gas gauge was touching empty, and so he said, "Coach, we had better pull over and get some gas." "No, no," keep going," Hayes replied.

Ferkany drove on as the gauge ventured toward the far side of E. He tried again: "Coach, we have to get some gas!" "We do not pull over and fill up!" Hayes exclaimed. "I won't buy one drop of gas in this state. I will push this car to the Ohio line before I give this state a dime of my money! The tax on the gas we pay for will just wind up supporting that football team up here, and that is not going to happen!"

So Ferkany kept driving amid visions of pushing that rental car through the snow. "We barely made it" across the state line, he said. "There couldn't have been a few drops in that tank."

Hayes' animosity extended beyond Michigan's football team. Center Jim Conroy related the story that in 1970 Hayes told him he would help him get into any law school he wanted -- except one. "I knew which school he meant, without him saying it," Conroy said.

The legendary coach didn't even want any symbolic reminders of Michigan around him. Linebacker Randy Gradishar tells the story that as the team was being introduced once at a Quarterback Club meeting, Hayes noticed that a freshman had on a blue tie. Right then and there, the coach "walked over and whipped [the tie] off that freshman. The crowd went wild."

You, too, have a story to tell; it's the story of your life and it's unique. No one else among the billions of people on this planet can tell the same story.

Part of that story is your encounter with Jesus. It's the most important chapter of all, but all too often believers in Jesus Christ don't tell it. Otherwise brave and daring Christian men and women who wouldn't think twice of skydiving or white-water rafting often quail when they are faced with the prospect of speaking about Jesus to someone else. It's the dreaded "W" word: witness. "I just don't know what to say," they sputter.

But witnessing is nothing but telling your story. No one can refute it; no one can claim it isn't true. You don't get into some great theological debate for which you're ill prepared. You just tell the beautiful, awesome story of Jesus and you.

It is true that Woody did not want to ever buy gas in the state of Michigan. I was a witness to it.

-- Ed Ferkany

We all have a story to tell, but the most important part of all is the chapter where we meet Jesus.

DAY 57

A ROARING SUCCESS

Read Galatians 5:16-26.

"So I say, live by the Spirit. . . . The sinful nature desires what is contrary to the Spirit. . . . I warn you, as I did before, that those who live like this will not inherit the kingdom of God" (vv. 16, 17, 21).

David Fathalikhani found success on the Ohio State baseball time -- at a position he never in his wildest dreams imagined he would or could play.

Fathalikhani came to Columbus in the fall of 2008 with intentions of walking on to the team as a catcher. He succeeded. "I just thought I could add more depth to the catching position, and work my way into some playing time," he said. "I never really fully expected to be a starting catcher."

He wasn't. He was redshirted in 2009 and then played behind All-Big Ten catcher Dan Burkhart in 2010. When Greg Solomon signed out of junior college prior to the 2011 season, his chances of getting any meaningful playing time were nil barring an injury.

But then Fathalikhani's college baseball career took a bizarre twist. Sometime before the start of the 2011 season, he went to the mound and threw a few pitches just for the fun of it. To his surprise, pitching coach Pete Jenkins liked what he saw. "We're going to put you on the mound," the coach told him.

Fathalikhani didn't hesitate. "Let's do it," he said, even though he had never pitched either in high school or Little League. "I just wanted an opportunity to help this team," he said.

Fathalikhani went to work and was so good at it that he made his first appearance on the mound in the second game of the season. He pitched a scoreless inning in the 8-7 Buckeye win.

Fathalikhani went on to be a successful middle reliever. In 2011, he appeared in 26 games with a 2-1 record and a 3.86 ERA. His success and his willingness to work to get better so struck his teammates that they voted him a cocaptain for the 2012 season.

Are you a successful person? Your answer, of course, depends upon how you define success. Is the measure of your success based on the number of digits in your bank balance, the square footage of your house, that title on your office door, the size of your boat?

Certainly the world determines success by wealth, fame, prestige, awards, and possessions. Our culture screams that life is all about gratifying your own needs and wants. If it feels good, do it. It's basically the Beach Boys' philosophy of life.

But all success of this type has one glaring shortcoming: You can't take it with you. Eventually, Daddy takes the T-bird away. Like life itself, all these things are fleeting.

A more lasting way to approach success, however, is through the spiritual rather than the physical. The goal becomes not money or backslaps by sycophants but rather eternal life spent with God. Success of that kind is forever.

I'm not content with the success I have had so far.
-- David Fathalikhani on pitching

Success isn't permanent, and failure isn't fatal --
unless it's in your relationship with God.

LIVE ACTION

Read James 2:14-26.

"Faith by itself, if it is not accompanied by action, is dead"
(v. 17).

What more can I say, man?" What more, indeed? Troy Smith had said it all on the field.

When the senior quarterback asked the gathered reporters his rhetorical question, he had just led the Buckeyes to a win over Michigan for the third straight season. This wasn't just any Big Game, however. This was the mammoth clash of 2006, the first game to feature No. 1 vs. No. 2 in the history of the rivalry.

By whipping Michigan 42-39, the Buckeyes finished the season undefeated, won the Big Ten, and secured a berth in the BCS championship game. In the biggest game of his career, Smith had also wrapped up the Heisman Trophy he would win officially three weeks later in one of the largest landslides in the award's history. He was the sixth Buckeye to win the sport's biggest personal award. (The others are Les Horvath, Vic Janowicz, Howard Cassady, Archie Griffin, and Eddie George.)

So when Smith sat down after the game, "turned his Big Ten champions hat backward, leaned on his elbows next to Buckeye coach Jim Tressel and smiled," he really didn't have anything left to say. After all, he had just become the first OSU quarterback since Tippy Dye (1934-36) to beat Michigan three years in a row.

Smith had spoken quite loudly by throwing for 316 yards and

four touchdowns in the game. One of the most exciting contests in the storied rivalry's history turned into what Tressell called "a fast-break game" and "Smith ran the anchor leg."

That "anchor leg" came with a long fourth-quarter drive. The Wolverines had scored to cut OSU's lead to 35-31, shifting all the pressure back to the Buckeyes in the process. Smith proceeded to lead the Buckeyes on an 11-yard, 83-yard, five-minute drive that effectively finished off the Wolverines. The clinching touchdown came on a 13-yard pass to Brian Robiskie with 5:38 to play.

What else was there for Troy Smith to say?

Talk is cheap. Consider your neighbor or coworker who talks without saying anything, who makes promises she doesn't keep, who brags about his own exploits, who can always tell you how to do something but never shows up for the work. You know that speech without action just doesn't cut it.

That principle applies in the life of a person of faith too. Merely declaring our faith isn't enough, however sincere we may be. It is putting our faith into action that shouts to the world of the depth of our commitment to Christ.

Even Jesus didn't just talk, though he certainly did his share of preaching and teaching. Rather, his ministry was a virtual whirlwind of activity. As he did, so are we to change the world by doing. Anybody can talk about Jesus, but it is when we act for him that we demonstrate how much we love him.

Jesus Christ is alive; so should our faith in him be.

Don't talk too much or too soon.

-- Bear Bryant

Faith that does not reveal itself in action is dead.

AT A LOSS

Read Philippians 3:1-9.

"I consider everything a loss compared to the surpassing greatness of knowing Christ Jesus my Lord, for whose sake I have lost all things" (v. 8).

Tom Cousineau believes he was the last OSU football player to see Woody Hayes alive.

A linebacker, Cousineau played for Ohio State from 1975-78. He set school records for tackles in a career, tackles in a season, and most tackles in a game (29). He was the MVP of the 27-10 win over Colorado in the 1977 Orange Bowl and was All-America his senior season. He was the first Ohio State player to be taken with the first pick of the NFL draft.

Cousineau was a captain of the 1978 team that ended the season with a loss to Clemson in the Gator Bowl. He saw his head coach deliver a blow to a Tiger player but didn't think much of it. "It looked like a small forearm and a push to me," he said.

He congratulated the Clemson players and then hurried into the locker room. "I changed and was out of there in about five minutes," he said. The next day he took a plane to Hawaii for the Hula Bowl, and "I was disconnected from the aftermath." As a result, he did not hear the news of Hayes' firing until he landed.

Years later, Cousineau said, "In the end, I loved the guy and I loved Ohio State and I always wanted to tell him that." So he did.

For some time, he had been carrying a large picture of Hayes around in his car trunk, and he stopped by the legendary coach's office one day to have him sign the photograph. Cousineau then told him "how much I cared about him, respected him, and how much he and Ohio State meant to me."

The next day, Cousineau's wife called and asked him, "What did you say to Woody Hayes yesterday?" Cousineau asked her why. "Well, he died today."

The loss was crushing to Cousineau, who has always believed he was the last player to see his coach alive.

Maybe it was when a family member died. Perhaps it wasn't so staggeringly tragic: your puppy died, your best friend moved away, or an older sibling left home. Sometime in your youth or early adult life, though, you learned that loss is a part of life.

Loss inevitably diminishes your life, but loss and the grief that accompanies it are part of the price of loving. When you first encountered loss, you learned that you were virtually helpless to prevent it or escape it.

There is life after loss, though, because you have one sure place to turn. Jesus can share your pain and ease your suffering, but he doesn't stop there. Through the loss of his own life, he has transformed death -- the ultimate loss -- into the ultimate gain of eternal life.

In Jesus lies the promise that one day loss itself will die.

To win, you have to risk loss.
-- Olympic champion skier Jean-Claude Killy

Jesus not only eases the pain of our losses
but transforms the loss caused by death
into the gain of eternal life.

DAY 60

DOOR PRIZE

Read Revelation 3:14-22.

"Here I am! I stand at the door and knock. If anyone hears my voice and opens the door, I will come in" (v. 20).

Thanks to a forgetful player, Woody Hayes once had an up-close-and-personal encounter with a dressing room door.

The 1951 season was Hayes' first as the Buckeye head coach. He started his career on a high note with a 7-0 upset of SMU. A pass from junior Tony Curcillo to sophomore wide receiver Robert Joslin and Vic Janowicz' extra point was all the scoring Ohio State could muster, but five interceptions helped the defense pitch the shutout. One sports writer commented, "Woody must have worked all summer on that game. He was really out to win the first one."

Ultimately, though, the season was less than satisfying for the rookie head coach as OSU finished 4-3-2. Hayes later said he was afraid he might be asked to resign since he was working on a one-year contract.

Thor Ronemus was a senior guard on that 1951 team. During the 16-14 win over Pittsburgh on Nov. 10, Ronemus came down with the flu. Trainer Ernie Biggs told him to stay in the dressing room after halftime and to rest. When he felt better, he could take a shower, dress, and go visit his family in the stadium. Biggs gave Ronemus the key to the locker room with careful instructions for him to get back to the dressing room with the key as soon as the game was over.

Ronemus forgot. When he finally did remember and made his way to the dressing room, he found the door had been smashed and torn off its hinges. Biggs told him Hayes had bashed it down to enter. A panicked Ronemus begged the trainer not to tell his head coach he was the one responsible for locking the team out.

Ronemus later said that every time he saw Biggs "until the day he died," he asked him if he had told Hayes yet. He never did.

You're all settled down in your favorite chair; your spouse is somewhere in the house; the kids are doing their homework or twittering. It's calm and quiet.

And then someone knocks on the front door. The dog erupts into a barking frenzy. Your spouse calls, "Can you get that?" You tell the kids to answer the door, whereupon they whine in unison, "I'm busy."

So you abandon your chair. A stranger, a friend, or a Girl Scout with cookies -- it makes no difference. You open the door.

How ironic and heartbreaking it is that so many people who willingly open the doors of their homes when anybody knocks keep the doors of their hearts shut when Jesus knocks. That's what Jesus does; he knocks at the door of your heart like a polite and unassuming guest. He'll step inside only if you invite him, but he's the one visitor above all others you want to let in.

The worst blowup I saw from Woody was when he knocked the door off the hinges to get in.

-- Robert Joslin

Jesus won't barge into your heart; he will enter only when you open the door and invite him in.

MAKE NO MISTAKE

Read Mark 14:66-72.

"Then Peter remembered the word Jesus had spoken to him: 'Before the rooster crows twice you will disown me three times.' And he broke down and wept" (v. 72).

Fumble, interception, fumble -- three quick mistakes and Ohio State had a landmark win over Notre Dame.

The Irish beat the Buckeyes in 1935 and '36 in the only two meetings between the traditional powers until 1995. Legend has it that Woody Hayes wouldn't play Notre Dame because he didn't want a second rivalry. John Cooper didn't like it either. "If you want to play us, come into the league," he said. "Why play them?"

But the schedule was out of Cooper's control, and he had games against the Irish in '95 and '96. That 1995 game didn't start out too well for the head Buckeye: He fell face-first leading his team onto the field. "I thought I was going to get trampled," he recalled. "I am not as fast as I used to be."

Well into the third quarter, the afternoon got longer for Cooper and his Buckeyes. The Irish led 20-14 and had forced a punt -- but that's when three Notre Dame mistakes proved decisive.

The return man fumbled the punt, and OSU's Dean Kruezer claimed it at the Irish 19. Three plays later, quarterback Bob Hoying hit Rickey Dudley with a TD pass. OSU led for good at 21-20.

Mistake number two was an interception following the kickoff. Cornerback Shawn Springs, the 1996 Big Ten Defensive Player of

the Year, pulled down the theft. Hoying then hit wide receiver Terry Glenn with a routine 12-yard toss that he turned into an 82-yard touchdown. 28-20.

Notre Dame fumbled again on the first snap after the kickoff for mistake number three. Matt Bonhaus recovered the bobble, and three Eddie George runs netted a touchdown. 35-20. The Irish couldn't recover from their mistakes as OSU won 45-26.

It's distressing but it's true: Like football teams and Simon Peter, we all make mistakes. Only one perfect man ever walked on this earth, and no one of us is he. Some mistakes are just dumb. Like locking yourself out of your car or falling into a swimming pool with your clothes on.

Other mistakes are more significant. Like heading down a path to addiction. Committing a crime. Walking out on a spouse and the children.

All these mistakes, however, from the momentarily annoying to the life-altering tragic, share one aspect: They can all be forgiven in Christ. Other folks may not forgive us; we may not even forgive ourselves. But God will forgive us when we call upon him in Jesus' name.

Thus, the twofold fatal mistake we can make is ignoring the fact that we will die one day and subsequently ignoring the fact that Jesus is the only way to shun Hell and enter Heaven. We absolutely must get this one right.

They made the mistakes and we capitalized.
-- Heisman-winning tailback Eddie George on the '95 ND game

**Only one mistake we make sends us to Hell
when we die: ignoring Jesus while we live.**

DAY 62

GOOD LUCK

Read 1 Samuel 28:3-20.

"Saul then said to his attendants, 'Find me a woman who is a medium, so I may go and inquire of her'" (v. 7).

It's hot out here, but it's got to be hotter inside of Ty Tucker's sweatpants." Yeah, but they were his lucky sweatpants.

The comment about the sweatpants and the heat came from a commentator during the telecast of the 2009 NCAA men's tennis championship in which the Buckeyes were the runners-up, the best finish in school history. The target of the wry remark was the Ohio State men's tennis coach, who has led the program to unprecedented success.

Before Tucker took the reins in 1999, the program had lost 24 straight Big Ten matches. From 2006-11, he guided the Buckeyes to six straight Big Ten regular-season and tournament titles. Tucker is so driven to win that for months after the 2009 finish, he kept the trophy boxed up. "I didn't want to look at it," he said. After all, it was awarded for second place.

Along with all that success, Tucker has brought his own brand of superstitions. Especially the sweatpants, which for years constituted the second-most "distinctive coaching garb" on campus, behind only the sweater vest of head football coach Jim Tressel.

Tucker wears them for every match. They are gray cotton, "the old-school kind Rocky Balboa donned while pounding slabs of beef in a meat locker." He wears only one pair each season,

BUCKEYES

washing them in local laundromats when the Buckeyes play back-to-back days on the road.

Tucker has other superstitions. The team no longer can eat at Olive Garden because they once lost a match after dining there. He has also burned a few of his so-called "lucky garments" after losses. He also places blue magic-marker dots on clothing labels so he never confuses his practice socks and his match-day socks.

Whatever it takes to help his team win.

Black cats are right pretty. A medium is a steak. A key chain with a rabbit's foot wasn't too lucky for the rabbit. And what in the world is a blarney stone? About as superstitious as you get is to say "God bless you" when somebody sneezes.

You look with a tolerant smile upon good-luck charms, tarot cards, astrology, palm readers, and the like; they're really just amusing and harmless. So what's the problem? Nothing as long as you conduct yourself with the belief that superstitious objects and rituals – from broken mirrors to your daily horoscope – can't bring about good or bad luck. You aren't willing to let such notions and nonsense rule your life.

The danger of superstition lies in its ability to lure you into trusting it, thus allowing it some degree of influence over your life. In that case, it subverts God's rightful place.

Whether or not it's superstition, something does rule your life. It should be God – and God alone.

Let's just say we've all got to do what makes us feel comfortable.
-- Ty Tucker on his superstitions

**Superstitions may not rule your life, but
something does; it should be God and God alone.**

IN THE KNOW

Read John 4:19-26, 39-42.

*"They said to the woman, . . . 'Now we have heard for
ourselves, and we know that this man really is the Savior
of the world'" (v. 42).*

Woody Hayes was so good at recruiting that he often seemed
to know things that sometimes befuddled his recruits.

Writer Jeff Snook said of the Buckeye legend, "It was as if he
had a network of private investigators working for him, telling
him when and where a recruit may be at any specific time." All-
American tackle Kurt Schumacher, who played for Hayes from
1972-74 and was inducted into the Ohio State Athletics Hall of
Fame in 2005, found that out when he was being recruited.

A friend of Schumacher's who was attending OSU had back
surgery. So her mother wouldn't have to make the return drive
alone, he rode with them to take her back to Columbus. Said Schumacher, "To the best of my knowledge, no one other than Jan, her
mom, and my family knew that I was making this trip."

Schumacher was thus totally dumbfounded when the three of
them walked into his friend's dormitory to find Hayes waiting to
greet them. The coach asked Schumacher if he had made all his
campus visits, and the recruit replied that he had. The coach then
cut right to the chase: He asked the high-school senior if he were
ready to commit to Ohio State.

Caught off guard and seeking to buy a little time, Schumacher replied that he would have to check with his sister, with whom he had lived since his parents' death when he was 14. Undeterred, Hayes strode to a pay phone in the lobby, dialed up Schumacher's sister, and handed him the phone. After a rather brief conversation, Schumacher told Hayes he was committing to OSU.

Hayes then invited the trio to dinner at the Faculty Club. To Schumacher's further amazement, they arrived to find a photographer from a local newspaper waiting for them to take a shot of Hayes and his latest signee sealing the deal.

Woody Hayes just knew about recruiting in the same way you know certain things in your life. That your spouse loves you, for instance. That you are good at your job. That a bad day fishing is still better than a good day at work. You know these things even though no mathematician or philosopher can prove any of this on paper.

It's the same way with faith in Jesus: You just know that he is God's son and the savior of the world. You know it in the same way that you know the Buckeyes are the only team worth pulling for: with every fiber of your being, with all your heart, your mind, and your soul. You know it despite the mindless babble and the blasphemy of the unbelievers.

You just know, and because you know him, Jesus knows you. And that is all you really need to know.

I never asked [Hayes] how he knew that I would be in the lobby of a girl's dorm on that night, and I'll probably never know.
                                                        -- Kurt Schumacher

A life of faith is lived in certainty and conviction:
You just know you know.

DAY 64

FACING THE MUSIC

Read Psalm 98.

"Sing to the Lord a new song, for he has done marvelous things" (v. 1).

Cie Grant got to sing one last time for his team.

Late in the summer before his junior season of 2001, Grant missed a portion of a team meeting, which meant a face-to-face with Jim Tressel to determine his punishment. The first-year head coach came up with a rather novel idea: Grant would sing "Carmen, Ohio" in front of the team.

What Tressel didn't know was that while Grant wasn't particularly interested in singing in front of his teammates, he wasn't exactly a novice. He had spent some time singing in his church choir when he was growing up. So he sang. He was good enough that the players coerced him into singing the song each Friday night before their next game.

When the national championship game in the 2003 Fiesta Bowl came down to the final play, it was Grant who got the defensive call: a blitz. "This is big, this is big, this is really big," he thought as he readied himself. Miami didn't have a tight end on his side, and he knew that the tackle opposite him couldn't block him. The stage was set for Grant to pull off what has been called "the most important quarterback pressure in Ohio State history."

"I got the best jump on that snap I ever had in my life," he recalled. He broke through and wrestled the Miami quarterback to the ground before he "saw that he didn't have the ball" and "didn't know what happened." What had happened was that he had pressured the quarterback into making a "homely pass [that] fluttered to the turf." The Buckeyes were national champions.

A few weeks later, on the bus ride to Ohio Stadium for the celebration of the title, the coaches and quarterback Craig Krenzel asked Grant if he would sing "Carmen, Ohio" one last time at the ceremony. Grant wasn't so sure; it was a big crowd, after all. Once his fellow seniors promised him they'd help out, he sang it and thus created one of his fondest memories of that magical season.

Maybe you can't play a lick or carry a tune in the proverbial bucket. Or perhaps you do know your way around a guitar or a keyboard and can sing "Carmen, Ohio" on karaoke night without closing the joint down.

Unless you're a professional musician, however, how well you play or sing really doesn't matter. What counts is that you have music in your heart and sometimes you have to turn it loose.

Worshipping God has always included music in some form. That same boisterous and musical enthusiasm you exhibit at Buckeye games when the marching band cranks up should be a part of the joy you have in your personal worship of God.

When you consider that God loves you, he always will, and he has arranged through Jesus for you to spend eternity with him, how can that song God put in your heart not burst forth?

It was cold and I hadn't warmed up my voice, but I am glad I did it.
-- Cie Grant on his final rendition of 'Carmen, Ohio'

You call it music; others may call it noise;
sent God's way, it's called praise.

DAY 65

YOUNG BLOOD

Read Jeremiah 1:4-10.

"The Lord said to me, 'Do not say, 'I am only a child' . . .
for I am with you and will rescue you" (vv. 7a, 8).

Howard Teifke wasn't old enough to be drafted, but there he was, playing football for Ohio State.

In the fall of 1943, the 17-year-old Teifke took a bus from his hometown of Fremont to Columbus. Young and green, he didn't realize the bus would drop him off near the Ohio State campus, so he wound up riding on into downtown Columbus and had to find his way back. Teifke was homesick right from the start. It didn't help that his uncle, with whom he was close, died soon after he arrived in Columbus.

Teifke wasn't the only youngster pressed into action for Ohio State during World War II; that '43 squad was so young they were nicknamed the "Baby Bucks." "The team was a bunch of kids that year," Teifke recalled, "because everybody else was in the war."

Only five of the squad's 44 players, all linemen with military deferments, were returnees from the national title team of 1942. The only returning starter was tackle Bill Willis, who would be inducted into the College Football Hall of Fame in 1971. He had volunteered for the army but had been rejected because he had undergone surgery for varicose veins.

Befitting its immaturity, the 1943 team is almost certainly the smallest in Buckeye gridiron history. Not a single player weighed

BUCKEYES

200 pounds. As a result, the equipment managers had a tough time rounding up an adequate supply of pants small enough to fit the backfield players, all of whom were 17 years old.

With only 44 guys on the team, Teifke, a center and linebacker, played a little that season. Like many of the youngsters, though, he turned 18 that year and when the season ended, he enlisted.

A lot older and much wiser after flying 26 missions during the war as a gunner in the air force, Teifke returned to Columbus in 1946. This time, he was among 220 players trying out for the team. He started both ways as a senior for the 6-3 team of 1948.

While our media do seem obsessed with youth, most aspects of our society value experience and some hard-won battle scars. Life usually requires us to spend time on the bench as a reserve, waiting for our chance to play with the big boys and girls. You probably rode some pine in high school. You entered college as a freshman. You started out in your career at an entry-level position.

Paying your dues is traditional, but that should never stop you from doing something bold and daring right away. Nowhere is this more true than in your faith life.

You may assert that you are too young and too inexperienced to really do anything worthwhile for God. Those are just excuses, however, and God won't pay a lick of attention to them when he issues a call.

After all, the younger you are, the more time you have to serve.

I was just a young kid lost in the big city.
-- Howard Teifke on his arrival in Columbus

Youth is no excuse for not serving God;
it just gives you more time.

DAY 66

IMPOSSIBLE DREAM

Read Matthew 19:16-26.

"Jesus looked at them and said, 'With man this is impossible, but with God all things are possible'" (v. 26).

It was a moment that had seemed impossible." That moment was a Buckeye lead. Yet there it was.

The 32-3 Buckeyes were ranked No. 1 and were the NCAA Tournament's top seed when they met Tennessee on March 22, 2007, in the first round of the South Regional. The Vols were a fifth seed and the definite underdogs. In the first half, though, the two teams switched roles. Playing "with more speed and no fear," Tennessee's "dominance was so thorough, you had to wonder how the Buckeyes were ranked No. 1 in the first place."

During that overwhelming first half, the Volunteers stormed out to a 49-29 lead. Only a three-point play from freshman David Lighty in the final second made it a 17-point deficit at halftime.

Just how impossible was Ohio State's situation? No team in the history of the NCAA Tournament had ever come back from that many points to win in regulation. That was impossible enough, but freshman stars Greg Oden and Mike Conley, Jr. were both in foul trouble and had already spent a lot of time on the bench.

Apparently, nobody mentioned the word "impossible" to the Buckeyes. They started the second half with a 16-5 run. Conley tied it up at 64 with a pair of free throws. When junior Matt Terwilliger hit two charity shots with 8:34 to play, Ohio State led for the first time in the "moment that had seemed impossible."

The two teams played even the rest of the game. Ohio State took an 84-82 lead on two Oden free throws with 1:38 left, but UT tied it with a pair of charity shots. The Buckeyes held the ball for one last shot, and when Conley drove off an Oden screen, he was fouled with 6.5 seconds left. He hit one, and Oden swatted away Tennessee's last-gasp attempt to save itself from what had once seemed to be an impossible defeat. The Buckeyes won 85-84.

Let's face it. Any pragmatic person, no matter how deep and abiding his faith, has to admit that we have succeeded in turning God's beautiful world into an impossible mess. The only hope for this dying, sin-infested place lies in our Lord's return to set everything right. In other words, pretty much start over again.

But we can't just give up and sit around praying for Jesus' return, as glorious a day as that will be. Such resignation runs counter to Jesus' instructions. Our mission in this cursed world is to change it for Jesus. We serve a Lord who calls us to step out in faith into seemingly impossible situations. We serve a Lord so audacious that he inspires us to believe that we are the instruments through which God does the impossible.

Changing the world may indeed seem impossible. Changing our corner of it, however, is not. It is, rather, a very possible, doable act of faith.

We knew if we took our shots, played our system, we'd be fine. There was a lot of time.
-- Mike Conley, Jr., on the possibility of winning the UT game

**With God, nothing is impossible,
including changing the world for Jesus.**

DRY RUN

Read John 4:1-15.

*"Everyone who drinks this water will be thirsty again,
but whoever drinks the water I give him will never thirst.
Indeed, the water I give him will become in him a spring
of water welling up to eternal life" (vv. 13-14).*

Ecstatic Buckeye fans tore up a chain-link fence, tore down the goalposts, and hoisted some players onto their shoulders. After all, the drought was over.

Despite one eleven-win season, two ten-win seasons, and two nine-win seasons, the Buckeyes had not been to the Rose Bowl for twelve years when the 1996 football season began. Thus, excitement ran high on Nov. 16 when they took on Indiana on the road needing only a win to make their reservations in Pasadena. The Hoosiers had lost fourteen straight Big Ten games, but that didn't keep them from playing Ohio State tough. As OSU wide receiver Dimitrious Stanley said, "People like to say they're not nervous in sports. Well, I was nervous the whole game."

The game was tied at ten midway through the fourth quarter when the Buckeye defense pulled off the big plays that ended the drought. With 6:18 to play, middle linebacker Andy Katzenmoyer popped the ball loose from the Indiana quarterback. Defensive end Matt Finkes snared it out of the air and took it in.

From there, strong safety Damon Moore took over. His fumble recovery set up what amounted to the game-clinching field goal

BUCKEYES

by Josh Jackson. He later returned an interception all the way to finish off the 27-17 win -- and the berth in the Rose Bowl.

Elated Buckeye fans partied on the field, even though they had to trample on a chain-link fence near one end zone to get there. When he met reporters after the game, head coach John Cooper, who had taken heat for prolonging the drought the previous three seasons, still bore lipstick marks from the celebratory kiss he had received from his wife.

You can walk across that river you boated on in the spring. The city's put all neighborhoods on water restriction. That beautiful lawn you fertilized and seeded will turn a sickly, pale green and may lapse all the way to brown. Somebody wrote "Wash Me" on the rear window of your truck.

The sun bakes everything, including the concrete. The earth itself seems exhausted, just barely hanging on. It's a drought.

It's the way a soul that shuts God out looks.

God instilled the physical sensation of thirst in us to warn us of our body's need for water. He also gave us a spiritual thirst that can be quenched only by his presence in our lives. Without God, we are like tumbleweeds, dried out and windblown, offering the illusion of life where there is only death.

Living water – water of life – is readily available in Jesus. We may drink our fill, and thus we slake our thirst and end our soul's drought – forever.

We'll pay for it.
-- Ohio State AD Andy Geiger when told IU officials were unhappy about the damage inflicted by celebrating Buckeye fans

Our soul thirsts for God's refreshing presence.

DAY 68

AD MAN

Read Mark 1:21-28.

"News about him spread quickly over the whole region"
(v. 28).

For Buckeye Jim Cordle, it paid to advertise.

Cordle was a three-year starter who began in 2007 as a center but finished in 2009 as a tackle. He even played some at guard. His sophomore season Cordle was listed by one NFL draft analyst as the No. 2 center in his class, but he disappeared from that list after switching positions.

Cordle first showed his versatility in 2007 when he injured his right thumb and had to wear a cast for several weeks. Offensive line coach Jim Bollman said he was worried that with the injury to Cordle the Buckeyes might have to scrap their shotgun formation. Coaches considered swapping him with guard Ben Person.

But Cordle told the coaches he'd take care of it and switched to using his left hand to snap the ball. Quarterback Todd Boeckman said the snaps were a little different at first because they weren't coming back as fast. Cordle got so good so quickly, though, that Bollman was soon crabbing anytime the snap was just a little bit off "just like you did with his other hand."

When the 2009 season ended, Cordle figured that his career of shuffling positions had left him in a position to be overlooked by the NFL scouts. He went to head coach Jim Tressel for advice, and the coach suggested he advertise. Cordle made a tape of twenty plays each with him at center, guard, and tackle and sent it to every NFL team. He also persuaded former Buckeye head coach John Cooper to vouch for him and land him a spot in the East-West Shrine Game.

The advertising paid off. He went undrafted in 2010, but during the 2011 season, the New York Giants were short a center. They remembered Cordle and signed him; he played in nine games.

Commercials and advertisements for products, goods, and services inundate us. Watch NASCAR: Decals cover the cars and the drivers' uniforms. Turn on your computer: Ads pop up. TV, radio, newspapers, billboards, every square inch of every wall -- everyone's one trying to get the word out the best way possible.

Jesus was no different in that he used the most effective and efficient means of advertising he had at his disposal to spread his message of salvation and hope among the masses. That was word of mouth.

In his ministry, Jesus didn't isolate himself; instead, he moved from town to town among the common folks, preaching, teaching, and healing. Those who encountered Jesus then told others about their experience, thus spreading the news about the good news. Almost two millennia later, nothing's really changed. Speaking to someone else about Jesus remains the best way to get the word out, and the best advertisement of all is a changed life.

I know I'm not the greatest player in the world, but when you're a three-year starter at Ohio State, you at least get a look.
-- Jim Cordle on advertising so he could get that look

**The best advertising for Jesus is word of mouth,
telling others what he has done for you.**

DAY 69

GOOD ADVICE

Read Isaiah 8:11-9:7.

"And he will be called Wonderful Counselor" (v. 9:6b).

All-American tackle Dave Foley had some stern advice for his good friend, backup quarterback Billy Long: "Long, whatever you do, don't throw an interception!"

For years, many experts ranked Ohio State's victory over Purdue in 1968 as the greatest in school history. When the two teams met on Oct. 12, Purdue was ranked No. 1; the 2-0 Buckeyes were ranked fifth, and Woody Hayes had a big surprise ready for the Boilermakers. As Foley explained it, the wily coach knew that Purdue's guys were big but they were slow. "So believe it or not, back in the third game of the 1968 season, we went to this no-huddle offense," Foley said. "The whole first drive, we get the ball and we never huddle."

They didn't score either, thanks to fumbles, penalties, and three missed field goals, but OSU dominated the scoreless first half.

In the third quarter, safety Ted Provost returned an interception 34 yards for a touchdown. Leading 6-0, OSU drove to the Purdue 14 in the fourth quarter when quarterback Rex Kern went down with an injured wrist. That brought Long into the game. "I've got spit hanging out the side of my mouth, I'm sweating and all that stuff," Foley recalled. "And the first thing I say to him is, 'Long, whatever you do, don't throw an interception!'"

He didn't. On his first play, Long dropped back to pass, and,

BUCKEYES

instead of trying a risky pass, he pulled the ball down when he couldn't find a receiver. He took off up the middle, and dragged two defenders across the goal line to clinch the 13-0 win.

"Suddenly, the Buckeyes were beginning to look like they just might be the best team in the nation." As it turned out, they were.

Like Billy Long, we all need a little advice now and then. More often that not, we turn to professional counselors, who are all over the place. Marriage counselors, grief counselors, guidance counselors in our schools, rehabilitation counselors, all sorts of mental health and addiction counselors -- We even have pet counselors. No matter what our situation or problem, we can find plenty of advice for the taking.

The problem, of course, is that we find advice easy to offer but hard to swallow. We also have a rueful tendency to solicit the wrong source for advice, seeking counsel that doesn't really solve our problem but that instead enables us to continue with it.

Our need for outside advice, for an independent perspective on our situation, is actually God-given. God serves many functions in our lives, but one role clearly delineated in his Word is that of Counselor. Jesus himself is described as the "Wonderful Counselor." All the advice we need in our lives is right there for the asking; we don't even have to pay for it except with our faith. God is always there for us: to listen, to lead, and to guide.

This is great, man. Way to listen to me, Billy.
-- Dave Foley's thoughts after Billy Long's touchdown

We all need and seek advice in our lives,
but the ultimate and most wonderful Counselor
is of divine and not human origin.

DAY 70

CELEBRATION TIME

Read Luke 15:1-10.

"There is rejoicing in the presence of the angels of God over one sinner who repents" (v. 10).

Two big-time basketball records fell -- and nobody paid much attention. No one had time to celebrate.

In 2011, Jantel Lavender completed what is most certainly the most spectacular career in Ohio State basketball history, men's or women's. A 6-4 center, she was the first player in Big Ten history to be named the league's Player of the Year for four straight seasons. She was a three-time All-America and four times All-Big Ten. She finished as Ohio State's all-time leading rebounder with 1,422.

On the night of Feb. 13, 2011, the Buckeyes took on Minnesota in Minneapolis. Early in the game, Lavender set an NCAA record by scoring in double figures for her 126th straight game. When the season ended, her streak had run to 136.

Lavender was on her way to 29 points that night, and nobody really noticed when she set that NCAA record. Everybody was too busy playing basketball. The game was tight to the finish with the added pressure on the Buckeyes of playing in "the noisiest and most wonderfully claustrophobic building in the Big Ten."

Early in the second half, Ohio State trailed 45-44. Lavender had scored 19 points in the game, which left her one shy of another big-time record: the school's all-time scoring record of 2,578 set by Katie Smith (1992-96). In 2002, the Ohio State Touchdown Club

named Smith the school's best female athlete of the 20th century.

Sophomore guard Tayler Hill pushed the ball up the floor and spotted Lavender open under the basket. With 16:28 to go in the game, Lavender hit a short jumper to set a new record. She went on to score 2,818 points in her career.

But in a game that had reached "the death-grip state of a sizzling second half," there was no time to celebrate. That came after Ohio State won 83-76.

Ohio State just whipped Michigan. You got that new job or promotion. You just held your newborn child in your arms. Life has those grand moments that insist on a celebration. You may jump up and down and scream in a wild frenzy at an OSU game or share a quiet, sedate candlelight dinner at home -- but you celebrate.

Consider then a celebration beyond our imagining, one that fills every niche of the very home of God and the angels. Imagine a celebration in Heaven, which also has its grand moments.

Those grand moments are touched off when someone comes to faith in Jesus. Heaven itself rings with the joyous sounds of the singing and dancing of the celebrating angels. Even God rejoices when just one person – you or someone you have introduced to Christ? -- turns to him.

When you said "yes" to Christ, you made the angels dance.

I didn't know. I wanted to keep the game on my mind and just play.
-- Jantel Lavender on breaking the school scoring record

God himself joins the angels in heavenly
celebration when even a single person
turns to him through faith in Jesus.

DAY 71

TOP SECRET

Read Romans 2:1-16.

"This will take place on the day when God will judge men's secrets through Jesus Christ, as my gospel declares" *(v. 16).*

During the famous "Ten-Year War," paranoia -- especially from Buckeye head man Woody Hayes -- "reached a level that would even make the era's Cold War participants shiver."

The Ten-Year War was the time from 1969-78 when Ohio State and Michigan played each other with Hayes and Bo Schembechler the respective coaches. Schembechler played under Hayes at Miami (Ohio) and was both a graduate assistant and an assistant coach for Hayes at Ohio State.

In the ten-year period the two men coached against each other, college football's greatest rivalry achieved an unprecedented ferocity. All ten times, the Big Ten Conference title was on the line.

The intensity of the rivalry also served to raise "the football drama from high art almost to high camp." For instance, Hayes always whispered in the locker room when his team played at Michigan Stadium because he was convinced Schembechler had bugged the place.

One time when he was watching film of a Michigan game, the head Buckeye noticed that the Wolverines wore a type of shoe he'd never seen before. Worried that the shoes might give UM an advantage on the field, Hayes found out what kind of shoes they

were and ordered that model for his team.

Perhaps the most outlandish -- and perhaps comical -- example of Hayes' concern over spies, secrecy, and achieving an edge involved some comely young women with obvious attributes. On a trip to Ann Arbor, Hayes ordered all the waitresses to leave the dining area during the team's breakfast. He was convinced that the attractive young women had been hired by Schembechler to distract his team from the game.

As Woody Hayes was about his football team's secrets, we have to be vigilant about the personal information we prefer to keep to ourselves. Much information about us -- from credit reports to what movies we rent -- is readily available to prying and persistent persons. In our information age, people we don't know may know a lot about us — or at least they can find out. And some of them may use this information for harm.

While diligence may allow us to be reasonably successful in keeping some secrets from the world at large, we should never deceive ourselves into believing we are keeping secrets from God. God knows everything about us, including every one of those things we wouldn't want proclaimed at church. All our sins, mistakes, failures, shortcomings, quirks, prejudices, and desires – God knows all our would-be secrets.

But here's something God hasn't kept a secret: No matter what he knows about us, he loves us still.

There aren't any secrets in coaching.

– Bobby Bowden

**We have no secrets before God, and it's no secret
that he nevertheless loves us still.**

DAY 72

POP THE QUESTION

Read Matthew 16:13-17.

*"'But what about you?' he asked. 'Who do you say I
am?'" (v. 15)*

Jim Tressel had two questions for team doctors: "If he gets
stitches can he go back in? Will it be a problem?" He got the answers he wanted to hear: "yes" and "no."

On their way to the 2002 national championship, the Buckeyes
opened Big Ten play at home on Sept. 28 against Indiana with
freshman tailback Maurice Clarett in the lineup. He had missed
the Cincinnati game the week before after having arthroscopic
surgery on his right knee on Sept. 17.

Clarett didn't appear bothered by the surgery or the layoff in
the first half as he scored on runs of 2, 1, and 4 yards and rushed
for 51 yards on 14 carries. The Buckeyes trotted off the field at the
break with a 21-10 lead.

Tressel and his coaches were definitely bothered when they
checked on Clarett's knee in the locker room and discovered that
it was bleeding around the incision. With a win far from a sure
thing, the head Buckeye wanted his freshman star in the game
even if it meant stitching the knee back up.

So he had those two pointed questions for the doctors. They
replied that Clarett could go back in and the stitches wouldn't
be a problem. As it turned out, they were right. After the doctors
stitched his knee up, Clarett carried the ball seven times for 53

more yards in the third quarter. He then broke a 28-yarder that was nullified by a penalty. When OSU put 17 points on the board in the third quarter to blow the game open (OSU won 45-17.), Clarett was through for the day.

His performance had answered not only Tressel's questions at halftime but all the questions swirling around his injury.

Life is an ongoing search for answers, and thus whether our life is lived richly or is wasted is largely determined by both the quality and the quantity of the answers we find. Life is indeed one question after another. What's for dinner? Can we afford a new car? What kind of team will Ohio State have this season?

But we also continuously seek answers to questions at another, more crucial level. What will I do with my life? Why am I here? Why does God allow suffering and tragedy?

An aspect of wisdom is reconciling ourselves to and being comfortable with the fact that we will never know all of the answers. Equally wise is the realization that the answers to life's more momentous questions lie within us, not beyond us.

One question overrides all others, the one Jesus asked Peter: "Who do you say I am?" Peter gave Jesus the one and only correct answer: "You are the Son of the Living God." How you answer that question is really the only one that matters, since it decides not just how you spend your life but how you spend eternity.

All of us in the stadium were excited to have Maurice back in uniform and playing. We're better when he's playing.
-- Jim Tressel on getting Clarett back on the field the last half

Only one question in life determines
your eternal fate: Who do you say Jesus is?

DAY 73

THE SUB

Read Galatians 3:10-14.

"Christ redeemed us from the curse of the law by becoming a curse for us" (v. 13).

One of the most significant single plays during Woody Hayes' 28 seasons" at Ohio State was made by a substitute who didn't even make his high-school team.

The Buckeyes of 1954 were 8-0 and were ranked No. 1 in the country when they hosted the 12th-ranked Wolverines on Nov. 20. With only one loss, Michigan could force a tie for the Big Ten title with a win and knock head coach Woody Hayes out of his first-ever trip to the Rose Bowl.

The Wolverines took the opening kickoff and drove 68 yards for a touchdown. They held on to that 7-0 lead for most of the half. Then came the big play by the unlikeliest substitute of them all.

With a little more than three minutes to go in the half, senior linebacker Jack Gibbs intercepted a pass. He was a second-teamer who had very little game experience and was on the field only because starter Hubert Bobo had aggravated a foot injury.

Gibbs, however, wasn't just any ordinary backup. After being told by his coach he was too small, he never even played high school ball. He graduated and worked for two years before enrolling at Ohio State. He ran across Hayes, who encouraged him to give football a try.

Gibbs had some talent and steadily moved up the depth chart.

He was expected to play considerably at fullback in 1953 until a broken ankle sidelined him. He returned for his senior season and had moved up to the second team by the Michigan game.

Thus, he was on the field to nab the interception. Quarterback Dave Leggett later hit end Fred Kriss for his first collegiate touchdown reception and the score at halftime was 7-7.

Gibbs' interception completely and permanently changed the game's momentum. The Buckeyes went on to win 21-7.

Wouldn't it be cool if you had a substitute like Jack Gibbs for all life's hard stuff? Telling of a death in the family? Call in your sub. Breaking up with your boyfriend? Job interview? Chemistry test? Crucial presentation at work? Let the sub handle it.

We do have such a substitute, but not for the matters of life. Instead, Jesus is our substitute for matters of life and death. Since Jesus has already made it, we don't have to make the sacrifice God demands for forgiveness and salvation.

One of the ironies of our age is that many people desperately grope for a substitute for Jesus. Mysticism, human philosophies such as Scientology, false religions such as Hinduism and Islam, cults, New Age approaches that preach self-fulfillment without responsibility or accountability – they and others like them are all pitiful, inadequate substitutes for Jesus.

Accept no substitutes. It's Jesus or nothing.

I never substitute just to substitute. The only way a guy gets off the floor is if he dies.
-- Former basketball coach Abe Lemons

There is no substitute for Jesus,
the consummate substitute.

DAY 74

ALL IN

Read Mark 12:28-34.

"Love the Lord your God with all your heart and with all your soul and with all your mind and with all your strength" (v. 30).

Tim Fox's enthusiasm for Ohio State football was dampened somewhat by his jersey number.

Fox arrived in Columbus in 1972 in a rather unusual position; he didn't have one. The Buckeye coaches had never seen him play. "I was surprised when they offered me a scholarship," Fox said. As a result, no one really knew anything about him.

The first day of practice was picture day. The coaches called for the freshman offensive backs to gather on one side and the freshmen defensive backs to collect at another spot. Like many good athletes, Fox had played both ways in high school, and since the coaches were unfamiliar with him, no one had told him where he would be playing.

So Fox asked assistant coach John Mummey where he should go. "Go where you want to go," he replied. Fox looked over to the offensive backs and saw Archie Griffin, Brian Baschnagel, Woody Roach, and a bunch of big fullbacks. He looked over to the defensive guys and saw only Craig Cassady. "I thought my odds were much better over there," he said. So he joined Cassady and played defensive back, one of the few Buckeye players ever given the chance to determine where he would play.

BUCKEYES

On that picture day, jerseys were handed out for the photos. They gave Fox No. 47, "and I was thinking how great this was." Until he looked around and saw two more 47s. "That dampened my enthusiasm," he said.

Only temporarily, though. Wearing jersey no. 12 (He never did wear that 47.), Fox was enthusiastic enough to be a starter his freshman season and each year afterwards. He was a team captain as a senior in 1975. The Patriots selected him in the first round of the '76 NFL draft and he had an All-Pro career.

What fills your life, your heart, and your soul so much that you sometimes just can't help what you do? We all have zeal and enthusiasm for something, whether it's Buckeye football, sports cars, our family, scuba diving, or stamp collecting.

But do we have a zeal for the Lord? We may well jump up and down, scream, holler, even cry – generally making a spectacle of ourselves – when Ohio State scores. Yet on Sunday morning, if we go to church at all, we probably sit there showing about as much enthusiasm as we would for a root canal.

Of all the divine rules, regulations, and commandments we find in the Bible, Jesus made it crystal clear which one is number one: We are to love God with everything we have. All our heart, all our soul, all our mind, all our strength.

If we do that, our zeal and enthusiasm will burst forth. We just won't be able to help ourselves.

If you are not fired with enthusiasm, you will be fired with enthusiasm.
-- Vince Lombardi

**The enthusiasm with which we worship God
reveals the depth of our relationship with him.**

THE FAME GAME

Read 1 Kings 10:1-10, 18-29.

"King Solomon was greater in riches and wisdom than all the other kings of the earth. The whole world sought audience with Solomon" (vv. 23-24).

Kirk Herbstreit is one of the country's most famous Buckeyes, but his fame has little to do with his time as an OSU quarterback.

As a senior in 1992, Herbstreit was a captain and the starting signal caller. He passed for 1,904 yards, led the Buckeyes to an 8-3-1 record and a No. 18 ranking, and was the team MVP.

A certain measure of fame inevitably comes with playing quarerback for Ohio State. Any fame that came Herbstreit's way for his on-field exploits, however, has long been eclipsed by his subsequent career.

As a college football analyst and a member of ESPN's *College GameDay* crew, Herbstreit is "arguably the most prominent pundit on the most prominent network for college football." Unintentionally, though, Herbstreit has achieved a level of fame usually reserved for rock stars and Hollywood leading men.

He usually has his own cheering section that chants his name when the crew takes a break. The GameDay bus was once pulled over by a state trooper who wanted to meet him. Sports show host Bruce Hooley has said, "When I travel with [Herbstreit], it's like traveling with [Bruce] Springsteen. People are constantly lunging at him to hug him, because they feel like they know him."

Such fame is far removed from the day in 1996 when ESPN promoted Herbstreit to the GameDay crew after one season as a sideline analyst. "When they hired me and unveiled me, I'm sure most of America was like, 'Who is this guy?'" Herbstreit said.

Not anymore.

Have you ever wanted to be famous? Hanging out with other rich and famous people, having folks with microphones listen to what you say, throwing money around like toilet paper, meeting adoring and clamoring fans, signing autographs, and posing for the paparazzi before you climb into your imported sports car?

Many of us yearn to be famous, well-known in the places and by the people that we believe matter. That's all fame amounts to: strangers knowing your name and your face.

The truth is that you are already famous where it really does matter, which excludes TV's talking heads, screaming teenagers, rapt moviegoers, or D.C. power brokers. You are famous because Almighty God knows your name, your face, and everything else there is to know about you.

If a persistent photographer snapped you pondering this fame – the only kind that has eternal significance – would the picture show the world unbridled joy or the shell-shocked expression of a mug shot?

Everywhere he goes, people love him. Women love him and men want to be like him.
– Radio personality Bruce Hooley on Kirk Herbstreit's fame

You're already famous
because God knows your name and your face,
which may be either reassuring or terrifying.

DAY 76

RUN FOR IT

Read John 20:1-10.

"Peter and the other disciple started for the tomb. Both were running, but the other disciple outran Peter and reached the tomb first" (vv. 3-4).

A dead bone in your feet is not exactly good news -- especially for a cross-country runner. In Molly Jacobson's case, it meant she had to walk again before she could run again.

Jacobson loves running. During her junior year in high school, she led her team to the cross country state championship, but noticed a weird and recurring pain in her left foot. After two visits to a doctor, she showed up at school on crutches and with a cast on her left foot.

The news was pretty awful for a runner; she had a dead bone in one of her toes. The recommended treatment was to stay off the foot, so she went months walking with a cast, then a boot with crutches, then with a walking boot. It didn't help.

Finally, the doctor recommended surgery. Without it, he said, the bone might well take up to five years to start growing again. That meant never running cross country again. Jacobson opted for surgery, which put her back in a cast and cost her preparation for her senior year of track and two family vacations.

"I was out of shape and my times weren't very good," Jacobson said about her final year of high-school running. When she didn't qualify for the state meet, her team didn't get to defend its state

title. "I was so frustrated," she said.

She considered never running competitively again, but Ohio State distance coach Chris Neal encouraged her to come visit the campus. In 2009, she walked on.

She had to work her way back into long-distance shape but by her sophomore season, she was one of the squad's top four runners. Continuing her comeback into her junior season of 2011-12, Jacobson saw herself as a role model to show the younger runners that "anything is possible as long as you want it and are willing to work hard."

Hit the ground running -- every morning that's what you do as you leave the house and re-enter the rat race. You run errands; you run though a presentation; you give someone a run for his money; you always want to be in the running and never run-of-the-mill.

You're always running toward something, such as your goals, or away from something, such as your past. Many of us spend our lives foolhardily attempting to run away from God, the purposes he has for us, and the blessings he is waiting to give us.

No matter how hard or how far you run, though, you can never outrun yourself or God. God keeps pace with you, calling you in the short run to take care of the long run by falling to your knees and running for your life -- to Jesus -- just as Peter and the other disciple ran that first Easter morning.

On your knees, you run all the way to glory.

I've learned a lot about myself and how much I love running.
— Molly Jacobson on the result of her injuries

You can run to eternity by going to your knees.

DAY 77

CUSS WORDS

Read Psalm 10.

"[The wicked man's] mouth is full of curses and lies and threats; trouble and evil are under his tongue" (v. 7).

Woody Hayes once encountered what he thought was a paragon of female virtue -- until she let loose with a string of profanity that may well have caused the salty coach to blush.

Defensive back Bruce Ruhl lettered for four years (1973-76) at Ohio State and started his last three. He was named to the Big Ten All-Academic Team in both 1974 and '75. In the 52-7 romp over Wisconsin on Oct. 12, 1974, Ruhl, playing safety, set a school record -- that has since been matched -- by intercepting three passes.

Jeff Snook tells the story of a trip Hayes made to a Detroit high school to recruit Ruhl. As Snook put it, Hayes was well known "for his love of America's wholesome values." Thus, he "hated long hair, free love, torn jeans, and the whole hippy-influenced ways of the late '60s and early '70s."

On the recruiting trip, as the coach and Ruhl strolled around the high-school campus, Hayes noticed a high-school girl walking toward him. As Ruhl recalled it, "She had on a pretty dress, had her hair done in a bow and all that."

Impressed by her appearance, Hayes said -- according to Ruhl -- something like, "Now see there, I guarantee you that girl comes from a good, wholesome family with good values. That's what we need more of in this country."

Just as the coach walked by her, though, a car drove by, hit a mud puddle, and splashed mud and water all over the girl. Ruhl said, "She suddenly let out a litany of profanity, screaming every bad word in the book."

As Ruhl recounts it, "Woody just continued walking and never said a word."

Whether we like it or not, we live today in a coarsened culture where words no one would utter in polite society a few decades ago now spew from our music and our television sets—and our own mouths.

Honestly answer these indelicate questions: With what name did you christen that slow driver you couldn't pass? What unflattering words did you have for that stubborn golf ball that wouldn't stay in the fairway? And what four-letter words do you sprinkle liberally in your conversations with people whom you want to think of you as "cool"?

Some argue that profane language is really harmless expression. It is in reality quite damaging, though, because of what its use reveals about the speaker: a lack of character, a lack of vocabulary, and a lack of respect for others and of reverence for God.

The words you speak reveal what's in your heart, and what God seeks there is love and gentleness, not vileness.

American professional athletes are bilingual; they speak English and profanity.

-- NHL Legend Gordie Howe

**Our words -- including profane ones --
expose what's in our hearts.**

DAY 78

TEARS IN HEAVEN

Read Revelation 21:1-8.

*"[God] will wipe every tear from their eyes. There will be
no more death or mourning or crying or pain" (v. 4).*

Andy Groom couldn't help it; he just broke down and, as he put
it, cried like a baby. It wasn't the only time that postseason.

A senior, Groom was the walk-on punter for the 2002 national
champs. He averaged 45 yards a kick that season and was named
to several All-America teams.

For Groom, the season ended in tears. He was careful to take
in everything about the Fiesta Bowl, "so I would remember it the
rest of my life." When the game ended, though, his immediate
reaction was bittersweet tears. He was overjoyed because of what
his team had just accomplished, but he was saddened because
his time as a Buckeye was over.

It wasn't the only time Groom found himself in tears after the
season ended. Weeks later at the celebration in Ohio Stadium, he
really broke down. "It was a very emotional day to have all of us
come together as a team for the last time," he admitted. Being with
his fellow seniors, dotting the *I*, and listening to linebacker Cie
Grant sing "Carmen, Ohio" (See Devotion No. 64.), all conspired
to wreak havoc with Groom's poise.

But there was an additional factor that pushed him over the
edge. For the first time in his life, he saw his father cry. "All of that,"
he said, "was too much for me to absorb all at once, and I began to

cry like a baby. It was so hard to say good-bye to something that I [had] known and loved for so much of my life."

Groom did have one more exciting postseason moment that didn't involve tears. Just moments before the team met the president on the traditional trip to the White House, head coach Jim Tressel pulled him aside and said, "Groomy, you're my man." The punter had no idea what his coach was talking about, but Tressel had picked him to present a team helmet to the president.

When your parents died. When a friend told you she was divorcing. When you broke your collarbone. When you watch a sad movie. You cry.

Crying is as much a part of life as are breathing, bad fast food, and potholes on the highway. Usually our tears are brought on by pain, sorrow, or disappointment.

But what about when your child was born? When Ohio State beats Michigan? When you discovered Jesus Christ? Those times elicit tears too; as Andy Groom did twice after the national title, we cry at the times of our greatest, most overwhelming joy.

Thus, while there will be tears in Heaven, they will only be tears of sheer, unmitigated, undiluted joy. The greatest joy possible, a joy beyond our imagining, must occur when we finally see Christ. If we shed tears when OSU wins a game, can we really believe that we will stand dry-eyed and calm in the presence of Jesus?

What we will not shed in Heaven are tears of sorrow and pain.

I just sat down and cried, because I knew what we had done was special.
-- Andy Groom at the end of the 2003 Fiesta Bowl

Tears in Heaven will be like everything else there:
a part of the joy we will experience.

WORK ETHIC

Read Matthew 9:35-38.

"Then he said to his disciples, 'The harvest is plentiful but the workers are few. Ask the Lord of the harvest, therefore, to send out workers into his harvest field'" (vv. 37-38).

Evan Turner left Ohio State after the 2009-10 season as the best basketball player in the country, but he didn't arrive in Columbus that way. Hard work accounted for the change.

From the spring of 2008 through the summer of 2009, Buckeye team manager Lee Miller got the same three-word text at night, sometimes after 10 p.m.: "Want to shoot?" He sometimes tried to beg off by noting he didn't have a ride, but the offer of one always came. So the two students would meet up and head for the gym.

There, Miller rebounded and fired back passes to the shooter. Or he played defense. Or just watched as his courtmate dribbled two balls at once, created spin moves, or did crossovers with his eyes closed. Always, that player was "working his game and his imagination until he'd reached 35 points."

That wasn't just occasionally either. It was usually six nights a week in the spring and the summer.

That player was Evan Turner, who, in his junior season of 2009-10, was the best college basketball player in the country. That season he led the Buckeyes to the league's cochampionship, a 29-8 record, and a berth in the Sweet Sixteen. He swept nearly all of the major player of the year awards and was the Big Ten's male

Athlete of the Year.

But that recognition came after all those late nights in the gym his freshman and sophomore seasons when Turner was driven to hard work because he knew he wasn't good enough. "My first two or three months [at Ohio State]," he said, "I didn't know if I could play at this level. . . . I wasn't sure of myself."

So he went to work and became what OSU head coach Thad Matta called "a poster child for young players." "This is how you do it," the coach said. You work for it.

Do you embrace hard work or try to avoid it? No matter how hard you may try, you really can't escape hard work. Funny thing about all these labor-saving devices like cell phones and laptop computers: You're working longer and harder than ever. For many of us, our work defines us perhaps more than any other aspect of our lives. But there's a workforce you're a part of that doesn't show up in any Labor Department statistics or any IRS records.

You're part of God's staff; God has a specific job that only you can do for him. It's often referred to as a "calling," but it amounts to your serving God where there is a need in the way that best suits your God-given abilities and talents

You should stand ready to work for God all the time, 24-7. Those are awful hours, but the benefits are out of this world.

When a lot of players around the country were out having a good time, I was working. It was like therapy to me.
— Evan Turner

God calls you to work for him using the talents
and gifts he gave you; whether you're a worker
or a malingerer is up to you.

DAY 80

STRANGE BUT TRUE

Read Philippians 2:1-11.

"And being found in appearance as a man, he humbled himself and became obedient to death -- even death on a cross!" (v. 7)

Strange but true: Ohio State once won a football game with some of the Buckeye players standing on the sideline in their street clothes and many of the fans on their way home.

A year after winning the national championship, the Buckeyes of Coach Paul Brown appeared to have tied Illinois 26-26 in 1943. When the final horn sounded, players of both teams headed for the dressing room, and fans fled for the exits. Only a few folks seemed to notice the officials' conference. Even fewer had spotted the flag the head linesman had thrown on the last play of the game. Illinois had been offside.

Such confusion reigned that after the refs decided Ohio State would get one last play, they really didn't know where the ball should be placed. They finally decided on the 18-yard line.

The officials then had the problem of getting the teams back onto the field. More than a few of the players from both squads were already in the showers. Many of them simply and hurriedly donned street clothes and walked back to the sideline to watch the game's second ending. After some twelve minutes had passed, the refs blew the whistle for the last play.

The strangeness continued when Brown ordered John Stungis,

the team's 18-year-old freshman quarterback, to try a 35-yard field goal. Stungis had never attempted a place kick before. His kick was good, and Ohio State won 29-26 in what became known as the "Fifth Quarter" win.

Many of the spectators who had left the stadium with the score tied did not learn until they read the Sunday newspapers that the Buckeyes had won in one of the strangest endings in Ohio State football history.

Life is just strange, isn't it? How else to explain the college bowl situation, Dr. Phil, tattoos, curling, tofu, and teenagers? Isn't it strange that today we have more ways to stay in touch with each other yet are losing the intimacy of personal contact?

And how strange is God's plan to save us? Think a minute about what God did. He could have come roaring down, destroying and blasting everyone whose sinfulness offended him, which, of course, is pretty much all of us. Then he could have brushed off his hands, nodded the divine head, and left a scorched planet in his wake. All in a day's work.

Instead, God came up with a totally novel plan: He would save the world by becoming a human being, letting himself be humiliated, tortured, and killed, thus establishing a kingdom of justice and righteousness that will last forever.

It's a strange way to save the world – but it's true.

Most of us had taken our uniforms off when they made us come back on the field. We couldn't believe it. It was amazing.
-- OSU Center Howard Teifke on the '43 Illinois game

**It's strange but true: God allowed himself
to be killed on a cross to save the world.**

DAY 81

TOLD YOU SO

Read Matthew 24:15-31.

"See, I have told you ahead of time" (v. 25).

Jim DeLeone quite proudly and intentionally said to his head coach, "I told you I would do it."

Earle Bruce succeeded Woody Hayes as Ohio State's head football coach after the 1978 season. His first year he led the team to an undefeated regular season and the Big Ten crown. Only a one-point loss in the Rose Bowl kept the Buckeyes from the national title. Not surprisingly, Bruce employed and instilled many of the principles, philosophies, techniques, and attitudes he had learned as an assistant coach under Hayes from 1966-71, including the all-important ability to motivate his players.

In the winter of 1979 as Bruce settled in, he met with each of his players individually. Among them was DeLeone, a freshman center who stood only 5'10" and weighed in at only 210 pounds. Years later, DeLeone admitted that at the time, he "wasn't the best student, and I was a little wild." Nevertheless, he was unprepared for the blunt assessment Bruce had for him.

As DeLeone recalled it, "Coach Bruce looked at me and said, 'Son, you are not the type of athlete we are looking for. You are not big enough and you are a step slow.'" "I knew I wasn't big," DeLeone said. "Art Schlichter was bigger than me, and he was the quarterback, but I was the strongest guy on the team." So he bowed his back and told his coach, "I will make you eat your words."

That spring, DeLeone occupied the bottom rung on the depth chart, and "they tried to run me off." But "they" couldn't. In 1979, he was the second-string center behind Tom Waugh, and in 1980 and '81, DeLeone was the starter.

After the '81 season ended, DeLeone told Bruce, "I told you I would do it." Bruce simply smiled in reply, apparently quite happy that his too-small and too-slow but motivated center had indeed told him so.

Don't you just hate it in when somebody says, "I told you so"? That means the other person was right and you were wrong; that other person has spoken the truth. You could have listened to that know-it-all in the first place, but then you would have lost the chance yourself to crow, "I told you so."

In our pluralistic age and society, many view truth as relative, meaning absolute truth does not exist. All belief systems have equal value and merit. But this is a ghastly, dangerous fallacy because it ignores the truth that God proclaimed in the presence and words of Jesus.

In speaking the truth, Jesus told everybody exactly what he was going to do: come back and take his faithful followers with him. Those who don't listen or who don't believe will be left behind with those four awful words, "I told you so," ringing in their ears and wringing their souls.

We'll win this game. I guarantee it.
  -- Joe Namath before the '69 Super Bowl, which his Jets won

Jesus matter-of-factly told us what he has planned:
He will return to gather all the faithful to himself.

OHIO STATE

DAY 82

KEEP OUT!

Read Exodus 26:31-35; 30:1-10.

"The curtain will separate the Holy Place from the Most Holy Place" (v. 26:33).

Woody Hayes once arranged a history lesson for his young football players by inviting one of the game's legends to speak to them after practice. The security guard wouldn't let him in.

Joe Menzer tells the story that after hearing the great Red Grange speak at a luncheon, Hayes invited the "Galloping Ghost" to deliver some inspiration to his players that afternoon. Grange played halfback at Illinois from 1923-25 and is still considered by many to be the greatest college player of all time. In 2011, the Big Ten Network named Grange the league's No. 1 icon.

Hayes, an incurable lover of history, had his excitement turn to frustration when he told his players who was stopping by later that afternoon and their reply was only blank stares. They didn't know Red Grange from Red Skelton. "How can they not know who this guy was?" Hayes fumed to his assistants.

When the appointed time for Grange's arrival came, however, he didn't show. The players went ahead with their practice while the head coach "kept glancing at his watch, nervously pacing as he waited for the big moment." Grange never did show up -- at least on the practice field.

The Ghost and his entourage did make it to the field's gate where the campus policeman guarding the gate pointed to the

BUCKEYES

"No Visitors" sign and refused to let them in. Grange protested that he had a personal invitation from the head coach to speak to the team. The guard said he had no personal knowledge of any such arrangement. "You can't go in," he repeated, obviously -- like the players -- having no idea who Red Grange was.

When Grange insisted, the policeman checked with an assistant trainer, who likewise was in the dark. The snubbed Grange turned away and left for the airport.

That civic club with membership by invitation only. The bleachers where you sit while others frolic in the sky boxes. That neighborhood you can't afford a house in. You know all about being shut out of some club, some group, some place. "Exclusive" is the word that keeps you out.

The Hebrew people, too, knew about being told to keep out; only the priests could come into the presence of the holy and survive. Then along came Jesus to kick that barrier down and give us direct access to God.

In the process, though, Jesus created another exclusive club; its members are his followers, Christians, those who believe he is the Son of God and the savior of the world. This club, though, extends a membership invitation to everyone in the whole wide world; no one is excluded. Whether you're in or out depends on your response to Jesus, not on arbitrary gatekeepers.

There are clubs you can't belong to, neighborhoods you can't live in, schools you can't get into, but the roads are always open.
-- Nike

**Christianity is an exclusive club, but an invitation
is extended to everyone and no one is denied entry.**

DAY 83

DREAM WORLD

Read Joshua 3.

"All Israel passed by until the whole nation had completed the crossing on dry ground" (v. 17b).

Matt Sylvester had dreamed about it and had even promised it would come true. When it did, though, he still couldn't believe he wasn't fantasizing.

Almost six years after the fact, Ohio State men's basketball head coach Thad Matta said he believed that what happened on March 6, 2005, was one of the biggest wins in his time in Columbus. The 18-11 Buckeyes hosted top-ranked and undefeated Illinois, a team that had hammered them 84-65 earlier in the season.

Sylvester, a junior forward, was the dreamer on the team who openly talked about beating the Illini with senior guard Brandon Fuss-Cheatham. According to Sylvester, "We said, 'Wouldn't it be unbelievable to score 25 points and hit the game-winner against Illinois? We literally said those words.'"

To everyone's surprise, the Buckeyes battled Illinois down to the wire. They trailed 64-62 with 12.1 seconds left when Matta, in his first year at OSU, called a time out and drew a play up for Sylvester -- just as he had dreamed.

Matta was confident. "I told our players, 'Gentlemen, we are going for the win,'" he said. Sylvester's reply had just as much bravado. "When I get it, I'm going to make it," he said.

A screen from junior forward Terence Dials, who as a senior

would be the Big Ten Player of the Year, freed Sylvester. Just as he had dreamed, he nailed the shot, a three with 5.1 seconds left that propelled the Buckeyes to the 65-64 win.

The upset kicked off an era of sustained success undreamed of since the early 1960s. Starting in 2005-06 and continuing through the 2011-12 season, the Buckeyes never won fewer than 22 games. The only year during that stretch in which the team failed to make the NCAA Tournament, they were NIT champions.

No matter how tightly or doggedly we cling to our dreams, devotion to them won't make them a reality. Moreover, the cold truth is that all too often dreams don't come true even when we put forth a mighty effort. The realization of dreams generally results from a head-on collision of persistence and timing.

But what if our dreams don't come true because they're not the same dreams God has for us? That is, they're not good enough and, in many cases, they're not big enough.

God calls us to great achievements because God's dreams for us are greater than our dreams for ourselves. Could the Israelites, wallowing in the misery of slavery, even dream of a land of their own? Could they imagine actually going to such a place?

The fulfillment of such great dreams occurs only when our dreams and God's will for our lives are the same. Our dreams should be worthy of our best – and worthy of God's involvement in making them come true.

I feel like I'm going to wake up suddenly and it's all going to be over.
-- Matt Sylvester on beating Illinois

If our dreams are to come true, they
must be worthy of God's involvement in them.

DAY 84

KEEPING THE PEACE

Read Hebrews 12:14-17.

"Make every effort to live in peace with all men and to be holy" (v. 14).

Led by their fiery head coach, the Buckeyes were ready to start a brawl after losing a football game -- until a heart attack.

In 1974, Woody Hayes assembled evidence that Michigan State was violating recruiting rules and blew the whistle on them to the NCAA. When the two met on Nov. 9, the Spartans led 16-13 with OSU sitting close to the goal line as time ran out. The Buckeyes hurriedly snapped the ball to beat the clock, fumbled it, and then were apparently saved when wingback Brian Baschnagel picked the ball up and ran into the end zone. "The referee called a touchdown, we thought we had won the football game, and we went to the locker room," Archie Griffin recalled.

But then the Big Ten commissioner showed up and told Hayes and his team they hadn't gotten the play off before the clock expired; Michigan State had won the game. Hayes exploded into one of his epic tirades. "I'm tired of these cheaters!" he raved. "They cheated me before in recruiting and now they've cheated me again!" Then he announced to his players, "We're going to go into their locker room and have a fight! I'm tired of this cheating."

That's exactly what the Buckeyes set out to do. A riot was clearly on the way, an incident "that surely would cost even Woody Hayes his job," as the Buckeyes followed their coach down a hallway to the Spartan locker room. Hayes flung open an outer door, fully intending to "burst into the Michigan State locker room to physically vent his hatred on this underhanded foe."

As the door opened, Hayes saw a longtime Michigan State employee running around and screaming in celebration of his team's win. Suddenly, though, the man grasped at his chest and collapsed. As others rushed to his aid, Hayes solemnly turned to his players and said simply, "Guys, we're going home."

Perhaps you've never been in a brawl or a public brouhaha to match what would have unfolded in the Michigan State locker room in '74. Maybe, though, you retaliated when you got one elbow too many in a pickup basketball game. Or maybe you and your spouse or your teenager get into it occasionally, shouting and saying cruel things. Or road rage may be a part of your life.

While we do seem to live in a more belligerent, confrontational society than ever before, fighting is still not the solution to a problem. Rather, it only escalates the whole confrontation, leaving wounded pride, intransigence, and simmering hatred in its wake. Actively seeking and making peace is the way to a solution that lasts and heals broken relationships and aching hearts.

Peacemaking is not as easy as fighting, but it is much more courageous and a lot less painful. It is also exactly what Jesus would do.

Run 'em over!
-- Woody Hayes to the team bus driver when some celebrating Michigan State fans blocked the vehicle's way after the '74 game

**Making peace instead of fighting takes courage
and strength; it's also what Jesus would do.**

DAY 85

JUST BY CHANCE

Read Luke 24:13-35.

"That same day two of them were going to a village. . . .
They were talking with each other about everything that
had happened. . . . Jesus himself came up and walked
along with them" (vv. 13-15).

Just by chance, a high-school player regarded as a middling prospect was in an office when a call came in for someone else. He got on the phone and subsequently changed Ohio State football history.

In 1991, Eddie George had an outstanding senior season for Fork Union Military Academy in Virginia, rushing for 1,372 yards and fifteen touchdowns. Nevertheless, the powers that be generally considered him to be a middle-of-the-road prospect whose future lay at linebacker. Only Louisville had offered him a scholarship as recruiting season wore on, but George wanted to play for a school with a richer football tradition than what the Cardinals could offer.

One evening, George was in his commandant's office when a phone call came in for the head man. On the line was Dan Osman, a former Fork Union cadet who was then a student trainer at Ohio State. When George learned who it was, he impulsively got on the phone and asked, "Hey, does Ohio State know about me? Tell them I want to come up."

Ohio State didn't know about him, but the next day Osman

mentioned George's name to recruiting coordinator Bill Conley. Conley followed up on the tip, later calling Fork Union and asking for some game tape. He liked what he saw. A few weeks later, Ohio State became the second school to offer George a scholarship.

The rest, of course, is college history. As a result of that chance encounter, George went on to win the Heisman Trophy as a senior in 1995 after setting a Buckeye record with 1,927 yards rushing. In 2011, he was inducted into the College Football Hall of Fame.

Maybe you met your spouse on a blind date or in Kroger's frozen food section. Perhaps a conversation in an elevator or over lunch led to a job offer.

Meetings and incidents that seem to happen by chance often shape our lives. Some meetings, however, are too important to be left to what seem like the whims of life. If your child is sick, you don't wait until you happen to bump into a physician at Starbuck's to seek help.

So it is with Jesus. Too much is at stake to leave a meeting with him to chance. Instead, you intentionally seek him at church, in the pages of your Bible, on your knees in prayer, or through a conversation with a friend or neighbor. How you conduct the search doesn't matter; what matters is that you find him.

Once you've met him, you should then intentionally cultivate the acquaintance until it is a deep, abiding, life-shaping and life-changing friendship.

Winners don't wait for chances; they take them.

-- *Unknown*

**A meeting with Jesus should not be a chance
encounter, but instead should be sought out.**

HERO WORSHIP

Read 1 Samuel 16:1-13.

"Do not consider his appearance or his height, for . . . the Lord does not look at the things man looks at. . . . The Lord looks at the heart" (v. 7).

Buckeye All-American Charles Csuri was a hero. He had the medal to prove it.

In November 2010, OSU head football coach Jim Tressel practically begged Csuri to join him at a New York press conference. The occasion was the unveiling of the Ohio State version of Nike's Pro Combat jerseys. Nike designed the jerseys to pay homage to the 1942 squad, which brought OSU its first national championship, and to the members of that squad who went on to fight in World War II. Csuri was one of those.

Csuri was reluctant to make the trip because at 88 he had a hard time getting around, but Tressel secured an ally in Csuri's wife. At the event, he spoke about his teammates while he stood next to a stagehand dressed in the uniform, which included a bronze star on the helmet and gloves with his initials printed on them. When someone pointed out the star and the initials to him, Csuri knew why Tressel had been so persistent. That uniform was a tribute to him in particular.

Csuri was All-America and the Big Ten's Most Valuable Player in 1942 even though he was the smallest tackle in the conference. He cleared lanes for running backs Les Horvath and Gene Fekete.

BUCKEYES

He was drafted into the army in 1943. At the Battle of the Bulge, he volunteered to take information to Allied headquarters. He ran across enemy lines in the snow; his helmet and his belt pack were both shot off during his trek. "You do things like that when you're very young," he said. "You think you're invincible in a way, or you can't conceive of your being killed."

For his actions, Csuri was awarded the Bronze Star for heroism. Thus, the star on the Buckeye helmet was a tribute to one of their own who was a bona fide hero.

A hero is commonly thought of as someone who performs brave and dangerous feats that save or protect someone's life – as Charles Csuri did. You figure that excludes you.

But ask your son about that when you show him how to bait a hook, or your daughter when you show up for her dance recital. Look into the eyes of those Little Leaguers you help coach.

Ask God about heroism when you're steady in your faith. For God, a hero is a person with the heart of a servant. And if a hero is a servant who acts to save other's lives, then the greatest hero of all is Jesus Christ.

God seeks heroes today, those who will proclaim the name of their hero – Jesus – proudly and boldly, no matter how others may scoff or ridicule. God knows heroes when he sees them -- by what's in their hearts.

It's one of those things that I did when I was very young, but I've long since forgotten about it.
                                    -- Charles Csuri on his heroic exploits in WWII

**God's heroes are those who remain steady
in their faith while serving others.**

DAY 87

THE GOOD OLD DAYS

Read Psalm 102.

"My days vanish like smoke; . . . but you remain the same, and your years will never end" (vv. 3, 27).

A basketball court that was too small. No locker rooms. No travel beyond fifty miles. The "good old days" of women's athletics at Ohio State weren't really that good after all.

Phyllis Bailey was a Professor of Physical Education for thirty years who "exerted a very strong influence in the development of women's athletics at Ohio State." In 1957, she was appointed coordinator for intramural and women's sports and by 1975 was Assistant Director of Athletics in charge of women's programs.

One year, Bailey sought permission for the women's synchronized swimming team to present their annual show in the full-sized natatorium in Larkins Hall. All she had at her disposal was a pool that she compared to a bathtub; it was only twenty yards long. Her request was denied because letting the women use the big pool meant "the men would have to put bathing trunks on."

In 1964, Bailey took the farsighted step of requesting that the women's so-called "sports clubs" be designated as true intercollegiate teams. To her surprise, the only response she received was "Do what you want to do." Nobody cared.

She had tryouts and thus began the modern age of women's intercollegiate basketball at OSU. The first game was played on March 6, 1965, a 33-19 win over Muskingum. The women weren't allowed to use St. John Arena, so they played in Pomerene Hall, a classroom building with no bleachers and a court smaller than regulation size. Not until 1973 did the women play in St. John.

Bailey's early teams also battled a widely held restriction that said "girls" should not travel more than fifty miles from campus for athletic events. Neither were those early OSU women athletes permitted to use locker or training rooms.

The truth is that "the good old days" for women's athletics at Ohio State are happening right now.

It's a brutal truth that time just never stands still. The current of your life sweeps you along until you realize one day you've lived long enough to have a past. Part of it you cling to fondly. The stunts you pulled with your high-school buddies. Your first apartment. That dance with your first love. That special vacation. Those "good old days."

You hold on relentlessly to the memory of those old, familiar ways because of the stability they provide in our uncertain world. They will always be there even as times change and you age.

Another constant exists in your life too. God has been a part of every event in your life that created a memory because he was there. He's always there with you; the question is whether you ignore him or make him a part of your day.

A "good old day" is any day shared with God.

At Ohio State early in the 20th century, there was a women's basketball team, but for years men were not allowed to watch them play.
-- *Abstract of Phyllis J. Bailey interview*

**Today is one of the "good old days"
if you share it with God.**

PROBLEM CHILD

Read James 1:2-12.

"Blessed is the man who perseveres under trial, because when he has stood the test, he will receive the crown of life that God has promised to those who love him" (v. 12).

Quarterbacks coach George Chaump told backup Kevin Rusnak to get into the game, but Rusnak had a slight problem: He didn't have a jersey or a helmet.

According to Jeff Snook, Rusnak (1967-69) "was a real character who loved to have a good time." For instance, on Christmas Day 1968 as the Buckeyes prepared for the Rose Bowl, he organized a sightseeing trip to Mexico despite strict orders from Woody Hayes not to cross the border. The group conned starting quarterback Rex Kern by telling him they were going to Disneyland. Naturally, Kern, wearing a sombrero, was the one who ran into Hayes as he tried to sneak into his hotel room.

Perhaps the crowning moment of Rusnak's carefree approach to life as a football player came in 1969 in his last game. As the clock ran down, Chaump told Rusnak Hayes wanted him to play in his last game. Rusnak then delivered a most unusual reply. "George," he said, "if you would have been here about two minutes earlier, I would have been more than happy to go into this game." But now he couldn't because he had a problem. He opened up his parka to reveal that he didn't have a helmet or a jersey.

It seems that a few minutes earlier, Rusnak had decided that he wanted to keep his jersey and his helmet as souvenirs of his playing days. He knew that if he went into the locker room with them, he wouldn't get to keep them. He spotted his girlfriend sitting three rows or so back and handed the gear to her. "Put this under your coat and make sure you get it out of the stadium," he told her. She did -- and thus Rusnak had a problem.

He never did get into that game.

Problems are such a ubiquitous feature of our lives that a whole day – twenty-four hours – without a single problem ranks right up there with a government without taxes, an Ohio State team that never, ever wins a game, and entertaining, wholesome television programs. We just can't even imagine it.

But that's life. Even Jesus had his share of problems, especially with his twelve-man staff. Jesus could have easily removed all problems from his daily walk, but what good would that have done us? Our goal is to become like Jesus, and we could never fashion ourselves after a man who didn't encounter job stress, criticism, loneliness, temptation, frustration, and discouragement.

Instead, Jesus showed us that when – not if – problems come, a person of faith uses them to get better rather than letting the problems use him to get bitter. We learn God-filled perseverance and patience as we develop and deepen our faith and our trust in God. Problems will pass; eternity will not.

The problem with winter sports is that they take place in winter.
-- Humorist Dave Barry

The problem with problems is that
we often let them use us and become bitter
rather than using them to become better.

DAY 89

GOOD SPORTS

Read Titus 2:1-8.

"Show integrity, seriousness and soundness of speech that cannot be condemned, so that those who oppose you may be ashamed because they have nothing bad to say about us" (vv. 7b, 8).

After edging Wisconsin in a thriller, the 2002 Buckeyes traded postgame showmanship for postgame sportsmanship.

On their way to the national title, Ohio State was ranked fourth at 7-0 when the team made the trip to Madison for what everyone expected would be a barnburner. It was, so much so that when it was over, defensive tackle Tim Anderson called the 19-14 victory "certainly a quality win for us."

Wisconsin led 14-13 at halftime and then hung resolutely on through a scoreless third quarter. As they did against Purdue and Michigan, the Buckeyes rallied in the fourth quarter. On third-and-six from the OSU 16, Craig Krenzel lofted a long one to wide receiver Michael Jenkins, who battled two Badger defenders and came down with the ball for a 45-yard completion.

From there, OSU marched in for the winning score. Krenzel threw a 3-yard TD pass to tight end Ben Hartsock with 9:59 left in the game. "I was catching that with every part of my body possible," Hartsock said. "It was like there was a baby in there."

After the State defense stopped the Badgers, the offense took over with 4:29 left and ran the ball nine straight times. In the process, they ran out the clock.

The win marked the fourth straight time in the series that the visiting team had won. A trend had developed of the winners dancing at midfield on the home team's logo. This time, however, the Buckeyes opted for sportsmanship. Instead of dancing and insulting the Badgers, the players gathered at midfield and knelt in prayer.

One of life's paradoxes is that many who would never consider cheating on the tennis court or the racquetball court to gain an advantage think nothing of doing so in other areas of their life. In other words, the good sportsmanship they practice on the golf course or even on the Monopoly board doesn't carry over. They play with the truth, cut corners, abuse others verbally, run roughshod over the weak and the helpless, and generally cheat whenever they can to gain an advantage on the job or in their personal relationships.

But good sportsmanship is a way of living, not just of playing. Shouldn't you accept defeat without complaint (You don't have to like it.); win gracefully without gloating; treat your competition with fairness, courtesy, generosity, and respect? That's the way one team treats another in the name of sportsmanship. That's the way one person treats another in the name of Jesus.

One person practicing sportsmanship is better than a hundred teaching it.
-- Knute Rockne

Sportsmanship -- treating others with courtesy,
fairness, and respect -- is a way of living,
not just a way of playing.

DAY 90

WEATHERPROOFED

Read Nahum 1:3-9.

"His way is in the whirlwind and the storm, and clouds are the dust of his feet" (v. 3b).

The fallout from a game played in weather so bad that a portion of the tarpaulin froze to the field opened the way for an extended period of Buckeye gridiron glory.

The Ohio State-Michigan game of Nov. 25, 1950, has forever been known as the Blizzard Bowl. In five-degree weather, snow was pushed around by winds up to 40 miles per hour. The game was late starting because the ground crew had to cut up a $3,000-tarp that had frozen to the field it covered.

When junior guard Thor Ronemus hit the field for the first time, "I couldn't believe how bad it was. I had never seen a snowstorm like that." He remembered that many of the several thousand fans who hung around "would lose their footing and slide down the stadium steps toward us. As we looked up from the bench, it appeared as if people were coming down a water slide."

The statistics that day are inexplicable without factoring in the weather. Michigan didn't complete a pass or make a first down and had 27 yards total offense. Ohio State had 16 yards on the ground. The two teams fumbled ten times and punted 45 times.

"With wind, snow, sleet, and numb hands as handicaps," Vic Janowicz, who won the Heisman Trophy that season, kicked a 38-yard field goal in the first quarter for a 3-0 Buckeye lead. The ball

BUCKEYES

"went up on a cloud of snow. It just disappeared."

With forty seconds left in the first half, OSU led 3-2 when head coach Wes Fesler made a crucial decision to punt on third down rather than run out the clock. Michigan blocked the kick for the game-winning touchdown.

The 9-3 loss in the Blizzard Bowl "brought Fesler to a temporary state of depression" and he resigned. His successor was Woody Hayes.

A thunderstorm washes away your golf game or the picnic with the kids. Lightning knocks out the electricity just as you settle in at the computer. A tornado interrupts your Sunday dinner and sends everyone scurrying to the hallway.

For all our technology and our knowledge, we are still at the mercy of the weather, able to get a little more advance warning than in the past and that's it. The weather answers only to God. Snow, wind, and freezing temperatures will be totally inconsiderate of something as important as a Buckeye football game.

We stand mute before the awesome power of the weather, but we should be even more awestruck at the power of the one who controls it, a power beyond our imagining. Neither, however, can we imagine the depths of God's love for us, a love that drove him to die on a cross for us.

It was a nightmare. My hands were numb. I had no feeling in them and I don't know how I hung onto the ball. It was terrible out there.
-- Halfback Vic Janowicz on the Blizzard Bowl

The power of the one who controls the weather
is beyond anything we can imagine,
but so is his love for us.

WEATHERPROOFED   181

DAY 91

THE ANSWER

Read Colossians 2:2-10.

"My purpose is that they . . . may know the mystery of God, namely, Christ, in whom are hidden all the treasures of wisdom and knowledge" (vv. 2, 3).

Tom DeLeone had no answer for the question a Buckeye study hall coach threw at him. So he stayed around and became a two-time All-Big Ten center.

In the eighth grade, DeLeone went out for football and immediately quit "because it was a lot harder than I thought it would be." He went out again in the ninth grade and didn't even make his school's 90-man traveling squad. His sophomore year the senior starter got kicked off the team, and he took over at center. He played that position for the next 21 years.

DeLeone had a couple of highly recruited teammates, and when their films were sent around the country, some coaches started asking, "Who's that center?" Thus, he was recruited.

His father had died when DeLeone was 12, and when the first scholarship offer came in, his mother sat down and cried. Woody Hayes clinched the deal by talking about history for three hours with DeLeone and his mom in the kitchen of their apartment.

DeLeone arrived in Columbus in the fall of 1968 and was dismayed to see how many people were on campus. "Right there, I wanted to go home and pump gas," he said. One question kept him in Columbus. Study hall coach Jim Jones asked him, "What are you going to do when you get back there?" Other than pumping gas, which he really had no intentions of doing, DeLeone didn't have an answer so he figured he may as well hang around.

He started his sophomore season, was All-Big Ten in 1970 and '71 and went on to a 13-year pro career. In 2002, he was inducted into The Ohio State University Football Hall of Fame.

And it all really began when he didn't have an answer.

Experience is essentially the uncovering of answers to some of life's questions, both trivial and profound. You often discover to your dismay that as soon as you learn a few answers, the questions change. Your health worsens, your financial situation changes, one of Ohio State's teams struggles unexpectedly -- all situations requiring answers to a new set of difficulties.

No answers, though, are more important than the ones you seek in your search for God and the meaning of life because they determine your fate for all eternity. Since a life of faith is a journey and not a destination, the questions do indeed change with your circumstances. The "why" or the "what" you ask God when you're a teenager is vastly different from the quandaries you ponder as an adult.

No matter how you phrase the question, though, the answer inevitably centers on Jesus. And that answer never changes.

When you're a driver and you're struggling in the car, you're looking for God to come out of the sky and give you a magical answer.
-- NASCAR's Rusty Wallace

It doesn't matter what the question is;
if it has to do with life, temporal or eternal,
the answer lies in Jesus.

<caption>OHIO STATE logo with suitcase graphic</caption>

DAY 92

A FAST START

Read Acts 2:40-47.

"Everyone was filled with awe. . . . [They] ate together with glad and sincere hearts, praising God and enjoying the favor of all the people" (vv. 43a, 46b, 47a)

Ted Ginn, Jr., didn't get off to a fast start in his life.

Conventional wisdom has it that a man is born fast. Ginn, however, defies that wisdom. He started out pretty slow, at least for a football player at a speed position.

The first time anyone clocked Ginn he ran the 40-yard dash in a pedestrian 5.1 seconds. But, as he later said, "All my life, things have been thrown at me." A lack of speed was just another "thing" he had to tackle.

Ginn literally worked himself into a speed merchant. He used technical training on the track and weight lifting off it to increase his speed. As a junior and as a senior in high school, he was the Ohio state champion in the 110 high hurdles, running the fastest time in the nation his senior year.

Ginn was so fast that he was recruited to Ohio State by track coach Russ Rogers, who believed he could qualify for the 2008 Olympics. Ginn's first love, though, was football, so he put his track career on hold.

He made his mark at Ohio State as a receiver and a kick returner. In 2004 and 2005, he was first-team All-America as a returner. In 2006, he received the honor as an all-purpose player. He set a Big

Ten record with six punt returns for touchdowns. Conventional wisdom now accepted that Ginn was the fastest man in college football, clocked at 4.29 in the 40. He said his best time was 4.22.

His blazing speed was displayed for the whole country to see when he got the Buckeyes off to a fast start in the 2007 BCS title game. He gathered in the opening kickoff and simply blew past every Florida Gator on the field for a 92-yard touchdown.

That play, though, was also the one that slowed him down. On the ensuing celebration, he was injured and did not return.

Fast starts are crucial for more than football games and races. Any time we begin something new, we want to get out of the gate quickly and jump ahead of the pack and stay there. Our desire is to build up momentum from a fast start and keep rolling.

This is true for our faith life also. For a time after we accepted Christ as our savior, we were on fire with a zeal that wouldn't let us rest, much like the early Christians described in Acts. All too many Christians, however, let that blaze die down until only old ashes remain. We become lukewarm pew sitters.

The Christian life shouldn't be that way. Just because we were tepid yesterday doesn't mean we can't be boiling today. Every day we can turn to God for a spiritual tune-up that will put a new spark in our faith life; with a little tending that spark can soon become a raging fire. Today could be the day our faith life gets off to a fast start – again.

I wasn't born fast.

-- *Ted Ginn, Jr.*

**Every day offers us a chance to get off
to a fast start for Jesus.**

DAY 93

BEST FRIENDS

Read Ecclesiastes 4:9-12.

"If one falls down, his friend can help him up. But pity the man who falls and has no one to help him up!" (v. 10)

He arrived in Columbus known mostly as Greg Oden's little friend, but Mike Conley, Jr., left after having made a name for himself.

Compared to the 7-foot Oden, Conley, at 6-1, was little. Moreover, he had been playing basketball with Oden since middle school, so they were friends when they suited up for the Buckeyes as freshmen in 2006. But when pundits and fans spoke of "Greg Oden's little friend," they weren't being complimentary.

"I think people thought I was riding Greg's coattails," Conley said. That is, a whole bunch of folks figured that Ohio State recruited Conley in an effort to land his big pal.

But Buckeye head coach Thad Matta knew better. "The only two people that knew Michael Conley could play were myself and Greg Oden," he said shortly after the 2006-07 season began.

By then, Conley was tearing the Big Ten up, leading the league in assists and steals. His only real problem was his shooting: He wasn't doing it enough. Matta finally threatened to bench him if he didn't start shooting more often. Conley dutifully went out and scored 17 points in a win over Northwestern.

Perhaps Conley's biggest moment as a Buckeye came in the game against Wisconsin on Feb. 25, 2007, the 37th match-up of the two top-ranked teams in the AP poll. With the Buckeyes trailing by one and time running out, Conley spoke to his friend, telling Oden he felt like he would get the ball and make the shot.

He did. He hit a runner in the lane with 4.2 seconds left, and Ohio State won 49-48.

The two best friends led Ohio State all the way to the national championship game and then turned pro.

Lend him your car or some money. Provide tea, sympathy, and comfort him when she's down. Talk him out of a bad decision like going to school at Michigan. What wouldn't you do for a good friend?

We are wired for friendship. Our psyche drives us to seek both the superficial company of others that casual acquaintance provides and the more meaningful intimacy that true friendship furnishes. We are perhaps at our noblest when we selflessly help a friend.

So if we wouldn't think of turning our back on our friends, why would we not be the truest, most faithful friend of all by sharing with them the gospel of Jesus Christ? Without thinking, we give a friend a ride, but we know someone for years and don't do what we can to save her from eternal damnation. Apparently, we are quite willing to spend all of eternity separated from our friends. What kind of lousy friend is that?

The guy that gets overshadowed in this whole thing is [Mike] Conley because [Greg] Oden is such a super talent.
*   -- Iowa coach Steve Alford on Greg Oden's little friend*

**A true friend introduces a friend
to his friend Jesus.**

DAY 94

HOMEBODIES

Read 2 Corinthians 5:1-10.

"We . . . would prefer to be away from the body and at home with the Lord" (v. 8).

Vince Skillings' homesickness was perhaps the best thing to ever happen to him. It helped lead him to Christ.

From 1978-80, Skillings was a starter for the Buckeyes in the secondary. He was drafted by the Dallas Cowboys in 1981.

Only a day after a snowstorm his senior year of high school, he was walking home wearing only shorts and slippers when a car pulled over and an elderly man in the passenger seat asked him if he wanted a ride. Skillings pointed to his nearby home and declined the offer. The driver then introduced his passenger: Woody Hayes. "Was I surprised and embarrassed," Skillings said. "Coach Hayes must have thought I was a fool to be outside dressed the way I was."

But Hayes was on a recruiting trip. At the Skillings home, he asked Vince if he had something he could be doing. "I didn't come here to talk to you anyway," the coach said. "I came here to talk to your mother."

Four hours later, Skillings came back home, and Hayes asked him if he wanted to attend Ohio State. "With my mouth hanging to the floor," Skillings recalled, he answered, "Yeah, sure, of course." And thus was he recruited to Ohio State even though "I hadn't talked to coach Hayes for more than three minutes total."

In Columbus that fall, Skillings teamed up with fellow freshmen Leon Ellison and Cal Murray to become known as the "Three Musketeers." They went everywhere together. They also shared intense homesickness during the freshman preseason camp.

Skillings remembered that they went for a walk to get outside a little "and ended up downtown at some hole-in-the-wall church." God was in that church, however. Those three homesick young men gave their lives to Jesus Christ that day. "We came back all fired up and elated with a new outlook on things," Skillings said.

Home is not necessarily a matter of geography. It may be that place you share with your spouse and your children, whether it's in Ohio or Alaska. Or in Brenizer, Penn., as it was for Vince Skillings. You may feel at home when you return to Columbus, wondering why you were so eager to leave in the first place. Maybe the home you grew up in still feels like an old shoe, a little worn but comfortable and inviting.

God planted that sense of home in us because he is a God of place, and our place is with him. Thus, we may live a few blocks away from our parents and grandparents or we may relocate every few years, but we will still sometimes feel as though we don't really belong no matter where we are.

We don't; our true home is with God in the place Jesus has gone ahead to prepare for us. We are homebodies and we are perpetually homesick.

Everybody's better at home.

— Basketball player Justin Dentmon

**We are continually homesick for our real home,
which is with God in Heaven.**

DAY 95

BOSS MAN

Read Matthew 28:16-20.

"Then Jesus came to them and said, 'All authority in heaven and on earth has been given to me'" (v. 18).

Joe Germaine didn't do what his bosses told him to, so he wound up with three secret service agents in his face -- and the president's autograph.

Germaine played quarterback for the Buckeyes from 1996-98, splitting time with Stanley Jackson for two seasons and taking over as the sole starter in 1998. He set twelve school passing records, including most passing yards in a season and completions in a season. In the 1997 Rose Bowl against Arizona State, he tossed the game-winning touchdown and was named the game's MVP. He was also the Big Ten MVP in '98; in 2000, he was named to the Ohio State Football All-Century Team.

Germaine was redshirted in 1995. One Friday that year President Bill Clinton appeared on campus to deliver a speech. The coaches gave the players very precise instructions about where and how they could greet the president. They specifically told the players not to take anything with them.

Later, when Germaine learned that President Clinton was on the move, he hurried out to meet him. On the way, he realized he was carrying a football, so he tucked it under his shirt. On the street, the president left his car and moved into the crowd to meet and greet. "I didn't know what to do with this football," Ger-

maine recalled, "but I pulled it out." He was promptly surrounded by three scowling and quite unhappy secret service agents.

The president was unperturbed. "Oh, you want me to sign that?" he asked. He did and then had Vice-President Al Gore sign the ball before it went back to the Buckeye quarterback.

Because Germaine didn't follow his bosses' orders, he had a memory and a souvenir – and a most uncomfortable moment.

No matter what our line of work may be, we all have bosses; even if we're self-employed, we work for our customers or clients. One of the key aspects of being an effective boss is spelling out in detail exactly what is expected of those whom the boss directs.

Wouldn't it be helpful if our faith life worked that way, too? Wouldn't it be wonderful if we had a boss who tells us exactly what we are to do? Well, we do.

For Christians, our boss is Jesus, the one to whom all authority on this Earth has been given. As the king of the world, Jesus is the grandest and biggest boss of all. The last thing that boss did before he left us for a while was to deliver a set of instructions. Jesus told us we are to do three things: 1) go and make disciples everywhere; 2) baptize those disciples; and 3) teach those disciples.

There we have it, straight from the head man's mouth just as clear and as precise as we could want it. The real question is how well we are following our boss's instructions.

The coach should be the absolute boss, but he still should maintain an open mind.
-- Boston Celtics legend Red Auerbach

The king of the world is our boss,
and he has told us exactly what he wants us to do.

DAY 96

CLOCKWORK

Read Matthew 25:1-13.

"Keep watch, because you do not know the day or the hour" (v. 13).

Ray Small was so fast he stopped the clock.

On their way to an 11-2 record and a win over Oregon in the Rose Bowl, the Buckeyes of 2009 throttled Wisconsin 31-13 on Oct. 10 in the Horseshoe. They didn't do it in typical Buckeye fashion; that is, they didn't grind the Badgers into submission. Rather, they stunned them into defeat with three big plays that were really all they needed.

Strong safety Kurt Coleman made the first one. He returned an interception 89 yards in the first quarter, enlivening what had been a "stale exchange of punts" and giving the Buckeyes a 7-0 lead. "As soon as I caught it, I saw a sea of red, and I was headed to the sideline," Coleman said. "I turned on my miniboosters. . . . I knew that no one was going to be able to catch me."

Free safety Jermale Hines likewise used his speed to return an interception for a touchdown. "I got a couple of blockers in front of me and that was all," he said.

They were both spectacular plays helped along by pure speed. Neither play, though, was fast enough to stop the clock as Small did. Ohio State had a 21-13 lead when the third quarter began with Wisconsin's kickoff. Small gathered it in at the 4. "I was surprised they kicked it to me," he said. They shouldn't have.

He "burst out of the shadows of the Horseshoe and into the golden slashes of sun, loosening a tight game against Wisconsin with the kind of open-field speed that had not been seen at Ohio State" since Ted Ginn, Jr. Small basically found a little room between his blockers and took off. "He looked like he was shot out of a gun," head coach Jim Tressel said.

Ninety-six yards later, when Small had run out of real estate, his jets finally cooled. He seemingly had run so fast that he had defied time, none of which ran off the game clock during the touchdown. Time had apparently stopped.

We may pride ourselves on our time management, but the truth is that we don't manage time; it manages us. Hurried and harried, we live by schedules that seem to have too much what and too little when. By setting the bedside alarm at night, we even let the clock determine how much down time we get. A life of leisure actually means one in which time is of no importance.

Every second of our life – all the time we have – is a gift from God, who dreamed up time in the first place. We would do well, therefore, to consider what God considers to be good time management. After all, Jesus himself warned us against mismanaging the time we have. From God's point of view, using our time wisely means being prepared at every moment for Jesus' return, which will occur -- well, only time will tell when.

He took that thing and he downshifted and he was gone.
– Jim Tressel on Ray Small's kickoff return

**We mismanage our time when we fail
to prepare for Jesus' return even though
we don't know when that will be.**

DAY 97

THE PRIZE

Read Philippians 3:10-16.

"I press on toward the goal to win the prize for which God has called me heavenward in Christ Jesus" (v. 14).

The pressure of winning a second Heisman Trophy weighed heavily on Archie Griffin until one night he found peace while he was reading his Bible.

Griffin won the coveted prize in 1974 as a junior. "He's a better young man than he is a football player," Woody Hayes said about Griffin, "and he's the best football player I've ever seen."

Before his senior season even began, though, Griffin felt the pressure of winning the award again and thus becoming the first two-time winner. He admitted that even during the summer, "I used to think about [winning the Heisman again] all the time." He recalled Hayes' admonition that a player is either getting better or getting worse. "It was warped thinking on my part," Griffin said, "but I thought that for me to get a little bit better, I needed to win it again."

Griffin conceded, "I didn't need to be thinking that way," but he did until one evening he read Psalm 37:4 in his Bible: "Delight yourself in the Lord and he will give you the desires of your heart." Griffin took that verse to heart, and it led him to understand that he could not control everything and that he certainly had no control over how people voted for the Heisman Trophy. "All I could do," he said, "was go out and practice . . . and be prepared."

What the verse really told Griffin was that his job was not to win trophies but "to find joy serving God." If he did that, the Lord would take that pressure from him, and if it were the Lord's will, he would then receive the award as a gift.

At peace with himself, the running back's senior season went off without a hitch. Griffin won his second Heisman, still the only player in NCAA history to do so.

Even the most modest and self-effacing among us can't help but be pleased by prizes and honors. They symbolize the approval and appreciation of others, whether it's an All-American team, an Employee of the Month trophy, a plaque for sales achievement, or the sign declaring yours as the neighborhood's prettiest yard.

Such prizes and awards are often the culmination of the pursuit of personal achievement and accomplishment. They represent accolades and recognition from the world. Nothing is inherently wrong with any of that as long as we keep them in perspective.

That is, we must never let awards become such idols that we worship or lower our sight from the greatest prize of all and the only one truly worth winning. It's one that won't rust, collect dust, or leave us wondering why we worked so hard to win it in the first place. The ultimate prize is eternal life, and it's ours through Jesus Christ.

When I read that verse, it was like somebody lifted a big weight off my shoulders.
-- Archie Griffin on escaping the pressure of winning another Heisman

God has the greatest prize of all
ready to hand to you through Jesus Christ.

DAY 98

HEART OF THE MATTER

Read Matthew 6:19-24.

"Store up for yourselves treasures in heaven . . . . For where your treasure is, there your heart will be also" (vv. 20, 21).

Tom Ryan went with his heart and not his head, even when it left him sitting in his car sobbing uncontrollably.

Syracuse University, only a few hours from his hometown and the place where his older brother was already wrestling, offered Ryan a full wrestling scholarship out of high school. Accepting that offer obviously made a lot of sense.

Ryan's heart, though, was with the University of Iowa where he had attended wrestling camp almost every summer. The problem was that the Hawkeyes didn't offer him a spot on the team.

So Ryan went with his head and for two years lived with and wrestled with his brother at Syracuse. His heart, though, was still in Ames, Iowa. Thus, after his sophomore season in New York, he went with his heart, packed his car, drove to Iowa, and walked on to the wrestling team.

His first workout was a disaster. Two twin brothers "beat me unmercifully," Ryan remembered. He left that practice and went to his car in tears. When he settled down, he sat and contemplated whether he was willing to do whatever it took to succeed at this place where wrestling was really a tough challenge.

He decided he couldn't turn back. He compared his situation

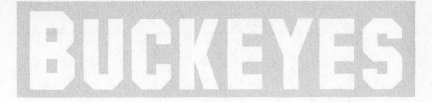

to the Vikings, who burned their boats when they landed on a foreign shore. His thought process was "there's no looking back."

Ryan stayed and was soon a starter and eventually a two-time All-America. He wrestled on Hawkeye teams that won Big Ten titles in 1991 and '92.

In 2006, Ryan followed both his head and his heart when he took over as the head coach of Ohio State's wrestling team. He led the Buckeyes to NCAA runner-up finishes in 2008 and '09 and was the National Coach of the Year in 2009. On Jan. 20, 2012, Ryan became the first OSU wrestling coach to beat Iowa since 1966.

As with Tom Ryan, we often face decisions in life that force us to choose between our heart and our head. Our head says take that job with the salary increase; our heart says don't relocate because the kids are doing so well. Our head declares now is not the time to start a relationship; our heart insists that we're in love.

We wrestle with our head and our heart as we determine what matters the most to us. When it comes to the ultimate priority in our lives, though, our head and our heart tell us it's Jesus.

What that means for our lives is a resolution of the conflict we face daily: That of choosing between the values of our culture and a life of trust in and obedience to God. The two may occasionally be compatible, but when they're not, our head tells us what Jesus wants us to do; our heart tells us how right it is that we do it.

I had this ache inside, and I just felt that the best way to cure the ache was to go [to the University of Iowa].
                                                                    -- Tom Ryan

**In our struggle with competing value systems,
our head and our heart lead us to follow Jesus.**

DAY 99

CLOTHES HORSE

Read Genesis 37:1-11.

"Israel loved Joseph more than all his children, because he was the son of his old age: and he made him a coat of many colours" (v. 3 KJV).

To honor their coach, who had been fired, the Buckeye players added an article to their uniform, one of which wound up in the College Football Hall of Fame.

Hours after a loss to Iowa and with the Michigan game still to be played, the decision was made in November 1987 to fire head football coach Earle Bruce after nine seasons. The result was that "perhaps no Ohio State team was more motivated to beat Michigan than the 1987 squad." They determined to give their coach one last victory ride on their shoulders; they also decided to pay Bruce a tribute.

Sophomore guard Joe Staysniak purchased headbands for the whole team and distributed them. Each player wrote "Earle" across his headband. They kept their secret until just before kickoff when, in unison, they wrapped them around their heads.

The gesture caught Bruce by surprise. During the coin toss, he recalled, "I look back there where the team is all lined up with their helmets off and something is on their heads." At first, he was miffed because "they know I don't allow that stuff." He strode closer to his players and saw his name on the headbands. "Well, I can't say anything about that," he decided.

The players then pulled off the upset. Matt Franz kicked a 26-yard field goal with 5:18 to play that was the difference in the 23-20 win over the Wolverines, Bruce's fifth in nine games. The headband-wearing Buckeyes then gave their coach a victory ride.

Bruce didn't have one of the headbands until a player gave him one before he was inducted into the College Football Hall of Fame in 2002. That headband wound up in Bruce's display in the Hall.

Contemporary society proclaims that it's all about the clothes. Buy that new suit or dress, those new shoes, and all the sparkling accessories, and you'll be a new person. The changes are only cosmetic, though; under those clothes, you're the same person. Consider Joseph, for instance, prancing about in his pretty new clothes; he was still a spoiled little tattletale whom his brothers detested enough to sell into slavery.

Jesus never taught that we should run around half-naked or wear only second-hand clothes from the local mission. He did warn us, though, against making consumer items such as clothes a priority in our lives.

A follower of Jesus Christ seeks to emulate his Lord not through material, superficial means such as wearing special clothing like a robe and sandals. Rather, the disciple desires to match Jesus' inner beauty and serenity -- whether the clothes the Christian wears are the sables of a king or the rags of a pauper.

We thought it was a great idea to honor a wonderful coach and a good man.
-- Linebacker Derek Isaman on the headband tribute

Where Jesus is concerned,
clothes don't make the person; faith does.

THE LAST WORD

Read Luke 9:22-27.

*"The Son of Man . . . must be killed and on the third day
be raised to life. . . . [S]ome who are standing here will . . .
see the kingdom of God" (vv. 22, 27).*

The Buckeyes in general and an All-American lineman in particular had the last word against North Carolina in 1972.

Archie Griffin (See Devotion No. 32.) was a rookie that season, the first one in which the NCAA allowed freshman to play varsity ball. He fumbled on his one and only carry in the season opener against Iowa. The Buckeyes recovered the ball, but Griffin immediately came out of the game. "Knowing how much Coach Hayes hated fumbles and wasn't real fond of playing freshmen, I thought, 'That's it. My season's over,'" Griffin recalled.

With two weeks to prepare for North Carolina, Griffin dedicated his practice time to making a good impression as a reserve. He had no idea he'd play against the Tar Heels; in fact, he was so convinced he wouldn't play that he didn't even stay in the hotel with the team the night before the game. Hayes surprised him, though, by calling for him to take the field. The stunned freshman had to scramble to find his helmet.

The Buckeyes needed a lift from somebody because they were struggling offensively. On the field that day was OSU tackle John Hicks, on his way to becoming a two-time All-America. As a senior in 1973, he won the Lombardi Award as the nation's most

BUCKEYES

outstanding lineman and the Outland Trophy as the nation's best interior lineman. Incredibly for an offensive lineman, he finished second in the voting for the 1973 Heisman Trophy.

As Hicks remembered it, "We weren't running the ball particularly well early in the [North Carolina] game." A defensive end came up to him and rubbed it in by declaring, "You guys up North can't block." Later in the game, as Griffin was setting a school record with 239 yards rushing and the Buckeyes were rolling to a 29-14 win, Hicks had the last word when he told that same end, "You guys from North Carolina can't tackle."

Why is it that, unlike John Hicks, we often come up with the last word – the perfect zinger -- only long after the incident that called for a smart and pithy rejoinder is over? "Man, I shoulda said that! That woulda fixed his wagon!" But it's too late.

Nobody in history, though, including us, could ever hope to match the man who had the greatest last word of them all: Jesus Christ. His enemies killed him and put him in a tomb, confident they were done with that nuisance for good. Instead, they were unwitting participants in God's great plan of redemption and gave the last word to Jesus. He has it still.

Jesus didn't go to that cross so he could die; he went to that cross so all those who follow him might live. Because of Jesus' own death on the cross, the final word for us is not our own death. Rather it is life, through our salvation in Jesus Christ.

The last word is in the field.

-- Pitcher Yadel Marti

**With Jesus, the last word is always life
and never death.**

NOTES
(by Devotion Day Number)

1   As early as 1887, students at . . . to get a real store-bought ball.: Wilbur Snypp and Bob Hunter, *The Buckeyes: Ohio State Football* (Tomball, TX: The Strode Publishers, 1988), p. 20.

1   He wrote Spalding's for a . . . how to kick the ball.: Snypp and Hunter, p. 21.

1   "Anything went except brass . . . attempt from four feet out.": Snypp and Hunter, p. 21.

1   It is safe to say that . . . both the students and citizens.: Snypp and Hunter, pp. 21-22.

2   Tears started to fill quarterback . . . "I couldn't believe we had lost,": *Greatest Moments in Ohio State Football History* (Chicago, Triumph Books: 2003), p. 213.

2   The Canes celebrated . . . up the Arizona sky.: *Greatest Moments in Ohio State Football History*, p. 213.

2   One referee hesitated because he . . . There's a flag on the field.'": *Greatest Moments in Ohio State Football History*, p. 213.

2   After security officials cleared the field,: Eric Kaelin, *Buckeye Glory Days: The Most Memorable Games of Ohio State Football* (Champaign, IL: Sports Publishing, L.L.C., 2004), p. 144.

2   "I'm bringing the juice,": *Greatest Moments in Ohio State Football History*, p. 214.

3   During a winter practice, . . . a whole new ballgame of pain.": Todd Avery, "Ohio State Pitcher Andrew Armstrong Overcomes 'Death Sentence,'" *The Lantern*, May 1, 2011, http://www.thelantern.com/sports.

3   During the summer, an othopedic . . . he did just that.: Avery, "Ohio State Pitcher."

3   "A lot of guys don't bounce back from that injury,": Avery, "Ohio State Pitcher."

3   It's like a death sentence to pitchers.: Avery, "Ohio State Pitcher."

4   That ranking rankled the . . . game's storied history, it rained.: Snypp and Hunter, p. 155.

4   In only one minute and 20 seconds,: Snypp and Hunter, p. 157.

4   After the game, Hayes riled up . . . marching band to Pasadena.: Snypp and Hunter, p. 159.

5   Why are we working on all . . . never run it in the games?": Jeff Snook, "*Then Tress Said to Troy . . .": The Best Ohio State Football Stories Ever Told* (Chicago: Triumph Books, 2007), p. 143.

5   Tressel prepared for Michigan the whole year.: Snook, *Then Tress Said to Troy . . .*", p. 143.

5   In his first season, (2001), Tressel . . . were doing it,": Snook, *Then Tress Said to Troy . . .*", p. 143.

5   Tressel used an unbalanced . . . Michigan off guard,: Snook, *Then Tress Said to Troy . . .*", p. 144.

5   on a play they had practiced but had not run all season.": Snook, *Then Tress Said to Troy . . .*", p. 144.

5   the Buckeyes used a play . . . for a 39-yard touchdown.": Snook, *Then Tress Said to Troy . . .*", p. 145.

5   None of the players ever . . . biggest game of the season.: Snook,*Then Tress Said to Troy . . .*", p. 145.

6   "I'm already writing my concession speech,": Joe Menzer, *Buckeye Madness* (New York City: Simon & Schuster, 2005), p. 111.

6   Cornelius Greene's thumb was swollen . . . "I have a plan,": Menzer, p. 109.

6   He said he believed his team . . . "If we're selected, we'll go.": *Greatest Moments in Ohio State Football History*, p. 102.

6   his realization of his unpopularity within the conference.: Menzer, p. 111.

6   Schembechler went ballistic, tearing up furniture at a press conference,: Greg Emmanuel, *The 100-Yard War* (Hoboken, N.J.: John Wiley & Sons, 2004), p. 104.

6   Hayes just smiled and call his wife.: Menzer, p. 111.

6   I just went nuts.: Menzer, p. 112.

7   "maneuvered [themselves] squarely into . . . and sold team memorabilia.": Peter Finney, Jr., "Terrelle Pryor, Buckeyes' Defense Shines," aolnews.com, Jan. 5, 2011, http://www.aolnews.com/2011/01/05.

7   [My quarterback] did exactly . . . lineman he didn't see.: Finney, "Terrell Pryor, Buckeyes' Defense."

8   "the world's greatest athlete of his era.": "The One and Only Jesse Owens Is Big Ten Icon No. 3," ohiostatebuckeyes.com, Feb. 14, 2011, http://www.ohiostatebuckeyes.com/genrel/021811aaa.html.

8   "No individual's accomplishments . . . those of Jesse Owens.": "The One and Only Jesse Owens."

8   the "seminal moment" for college track and field.: "The One and Only Jesse Owens."

8   "the greatest individual accomplishment in track and field history.": "The One and Only Jesse Owens."

8   "a landmark event in the . . . of the 20th century.": "The One and Only Jesse Owens."

8   [Jesse Owens] won four . . . athlete beyond question.: "The One and Only Jesse Owens."

9   "I remember I had . . . thinking the game was over,": Snook, *Then Tress Said to Troy . . .*", p. 33.

9   I was on the field . . . without the hip pads.: Snook, *Then Tress Said to Troy . . .*", p. 33.

10   "Anything that could go wrong went wrong,": Snook, *Then Tress Said to Troy . . .*", p. 119.

10   "That was probably the worst half I've ever been associated with,": *Greatest Moments in Ohio State*

![BUCKEYES]

10   *Football History*, p. 154.

10   "I told them to get out there and fight for their lives,": *Greatest Moments in Ohio State Football History*, p. 154.

10   "Sometimes you have to . . . back in the game.": Snook, *Then Tress Said to Troy . . .*", p. 119.

10   "To this day," . . . when they saw that game.": Snook, *Then Tress Said to Troy . . .*", p. 120.

10   "I still can't believe . . . of a football team,": *Greatest Moments in Ohio State Football History*, p. 154.

10   I didn't think there was any way possible they could come back.: *Greatest Moments in Ohio State Football History*, p. 154.

11   After his first game of '72, he started thinking about transferring.: Jeff Snook, ed., *What It Means to Be a Buckeye* (Chicago: Triumph Books, 2003), p. 139.

11   "It was a blessing in disguise," . . . I ran a counter.": Snook, *What It Means to Be a Buckeye*, p. 141.

11   Baschnagel had an 8 a.m. . . . walking back to his apartment.: Snook, *What It Means to Be a Buckeye*, pp. 142-43.

11   The two friends started a . . . in the third round.": Snook, *What It Means to Be a Buckeye*, p. 143.

11   I could have killed him.: Snook, *What It Means to Be a Buckeye*, p. 143.

12   When Cassie was growing up, . . . when we say 'Wolverine.'": Larry Watts, "Kicking Around All Options," *BigTen.org*, Feb. 4, 2011, http://www.bigtenorg/genrel/020411aaa.html.

13   Stanley noticed early on that . . . made the same promise to him.: Jeff Rapp, *Stadium Stories: Ohio State Buckeyes* (Guilford, CN: The Globe Pequot Press, 2003), p. 144.

13   The day before the game during . . . is where I scored,": Rapp, pp. 144-45.

14   As he arrived at a post-season . . . to play in the Rose Bowl.: Snook, *Then Tress Said to Troy . . .*", p. 52.

14   Hayes dropped his suitcase, . . . not their intelligence.": Snook, *Then Tress Said to Troy . . .*", p. 52.

14   The athletic board appealed to . . . to accept the decision.: Snypp and Hunter, p. 192.

14   I still don't understand it. . . . and they didn't let us go.: Snook, *Then Tress Said to Troy . . .*", p. 52.

15   forty candidates applied to replace . . . it past the initial screen,: Snypp and Hunter, p. 139.

15   Alumni, students, and a Columbus . . . sentence in the state penitentiary.: Menzer, pp. 33-34.

15   three-hour interview.: Menzer, p. 34.

15   Hayes didn't wait for questions . . . Hayes left confident: Snypp and Hunter, p. 142.

15   Gentlemen, I guess the hay is in the barn.: Menzer, p. 34.

16   Days was a high school star . . . "No, I want to play,": Michael Periatt, "The 1: Passion Propels Walk-On Eddie Days," *The Lantern*, April 4, 2011, http://www.thelantern.com/sports.

16   He was a practice player, . . . one of two free throws.: Periatt, "The 1: Passion Propels Walk-On."

16   It finally worked out.: Periatt, "The 1: Passion Propels Walk-On."

17   I'm outta here. I'm going to West Virginia to play.": Menzer, p. 66.

17   in practice he flattened quarterback . . . get to the guy with the ball.: Menzer, p. 65.

17   "Get this guy out of here!" . . . urged Stillwagon to stay.: Menzer, p. 66.

17   telling Stillwagon his parents . . . future star agreed to say.: Menzer, p. 67.

17   He might cool off, but I'm not going to cool off. I'm leaving.: Menzer, p. 66.

18   Larger crowds than ever . . . fans were showing up.: Snook, *Then Tress Said to Troy . . .*", p. 10.

18   "with a big heart and blazing speed": Snook, *Then Tress Said to Troy . . .*", p. 8.

18   "he was virtually untouchable . . . today's best running backs.": Snook, *Then Tress Said to Troy . . .*", p. 10.

18   By mid-season of 1917, . . . for the Wisconsin game.: Snook, *Then Tress Said to Troy . . .*", p. 11.

18   28,000 fans showed up for the game.: Snook, *Then Tress Said to Troy . . .*", p. 12.

18   The stadium was inevitable . . . playpen for the Buckeyes.: Snook, *Then Tress Said to Troy . . .*", p. 13.

18   Chic Harley put Ohio State football on the map.: Snook, *Then Tress Said to Troy . . .*", p. 13.

19   The senior defensive back was . . . going to happen to him.: Robert Gartrell, "Moeller Hoping to Finally Catch a Break," *The Lantern*, Oct. 21, 2010, http://www.thelantern.com/sports.

19   He hit his head . . . "Because I love it.": Gartrell, "Moeller Hoping to Finally Catch a Break."

19   Making a tackle, . . . what was wrong.": Gartrell, "Moeller Hoping to Finally Catch a Break."

19   I kind of thought . . . to happen eventually.: Gartrell, "Moeller Hoping to Finally Catch a Break."

20   "You just get hot,": Danny Restivo "Prahalis Reflects on 4 Years," *The Lantern*, Feb. 23, 2012, http://www.thelantern.com/sports.

20   "I don't look like . . . with China doll looks.": Jim Massie, "Unstoppable," *The Columbus Dispatch*, March 16, 2010, http://www.dispatch.com/content/stories/sports/2010/03/16/unstoppable.html.

20   In the seventh grade, . . . "She's a tough kid,": Massie, "Unstoppable."

21   in 1938 junior Ross Bartschy, . . . return the week before.: Snook, *What It Means to Be a Buckeye*, p. 5.

21   Head coach Francis Schmidt . . . other end of the bench.: Snook, *What It Means to Be a Buckeye*, p. 6.

OHIO STATE

21	he soon strode back to . . . go down to the other end of this bench!": Snook, *What It Means to Be a Buckeye*, p. 7.
21	The custom at OSU in . . . the crowd taking it?": Snook, *What It Means to Be a Buckeye*, p. 5.
21	When you run trick plays . . . folks question your sanity.: Jim & Julie S. Bettinger, *The Book of Bowden* (Nashville: TowleHouse Publishing, 2001), p. 32.
22	The one constant in Doss' life . . . business in Columbus was unfinished.: Kelley King, "Senior Moment," *Sports Illustrated Presents Ohio State Buckeyes* (New York City: Time Inc., 2003), p. 48.
22	he was simply having the best time of his life.: King, "Senior Moment," p. 46.
22	The day before the Jan. 11 . . . leave it in God's hands.: King, "Senior Moment," p. 49.
22	It started to get to me . . . to do at Ohio State.: King, "Senior Moment," p. 48.
23	He reminded them they had . . . they were the stronger team.: Tim May, "Season to Remember," *The Columbus Dispatch*, May 10, 2011, http://www.dispatch.com/content/stories/sports/2011/05/10/season-to-remember.html.
23	They had eleven kills . . . a perfect game offensively.: May, "Season to Remember."
23	We just overpowered them.: May, "Season to Remember."
24	documentation exists proving the Wolverine . . . the OSU-Michigan game of 1932.: Rapp, p. 92.
24	OSU's Department of Music had . . . after that 1932 game.: Rapp, p. 93.
24	when three Ohio State students . . . it to be "a pleasing combination.": Rapp, p. 92.
24	A group of students decided to . . . school had only 9,000 students.: Snypp and Hunter, p. 77.
24	the homecoming queen rode on her own float in the homecoming parade: Snypp and Hunter, p. 78.
24	her chaperones said she . . . in all the homecoming activities.: Snypp and Hunter, p. 77.
25	Horvath turned down some . . . and led the team in scoring.: Snypp and Hunter, p. 112.
25	With eight minutes on the clock, . . . drive all on the ground: Snypp and Hunter, p. 114.
25	"ambivalent, vacillating, impulsive, unsubmissive.: John MacArthur, *Twelve Ordinary Men* (Nashville: W Publishing Group, 2002), p. 39.
25	"the greatest preacher among . . . in the birth of the church.: MacArthur, p. 39.
25	[Leslie] Horvath had the personality . . . to almost unbelievable achievements.: Wilbur Snypp, *The Buckeyes: A Story of Ohio State Football* (Huntsville, AL: The Strode Publishers, 1974), p. 114.
26	When junior running back Beanie . . . "Don't pressure me anymore.": Doug Lesmerises, "Buckeyes Are Happy Campers." *The Plain Dealer*, Oct. 5, 2008.
26	An ESPN analyst had said . . . "a stage this vast.": Bill Livington, "Pryor Finishes on Stage with Panache," *The Plain Dealer*, Oct. 5, 2008.
26	"I made some young . . . had dwarfed the freshman.": Livingston, "Pryor Finishes on Stage."
26	The stadium was rocking . . . "Big drive,": Livingston, "Pryor Finishes on Stage."
26	"Rattled like his teammates . . . like a freshman": Lesmerises, "Buckeyes Are Happy Campers."
26	"This is a man's world,": Lesmerises, "Buckeyes Are Happy Campers."
26	We put it on [Pryor's] back . . . capable of doing it.: Lesmerises, "Buckeyes Are Happy Campers."
27	She was in chronic pain, . . . be there to watch her.: Graham Hays, "OSU's Pruner Finds Peace After Tragedy," *ESPN.com*, April 16, 2009, http://sports.espn.g.com/ncaa/columns/story?columnist=hays_graham&id=4073311.
27	"I couldn't even hold . . . how to explain it.": Hays, "OSU's Pruner Finds Peace."
27	Courtney hit one to heaven.: Hays, "OSU's Pruner Finds Peace."
28	All-American Buckeye receiver Terry . . . foot on a plane.: Snook, *Then Tress Said to Troy . . .*", p. 124.
28	He rarely traveled with . . . sleep than his teammates.: Snook, *Then Tress Said to Troy . . .*", p. 124.
28	"I didn't like to fly," . . . and then got on that one.: Snook, *Then Tress Said to Troy . . .*", p. 125.
28	the airport at State College, . . . then we'll go in.": Snook, *Then Tress Said to Troy . . .*", p. 125.
28	I am not flying. Can't do it. Don't ask me.: Snook, *Then Tress Said to Troy . . .*", p. 125.
29	"one of the least prolific in the Big Ten": *The Road to No. 1* (Texas Football/Epic Sports Corp., 2003), p. 97.
29	the Canes used the run to set up the pass.: *The Road to No. 1*, p. 97.
29	Pregame talk said it was coming right his way.: *The Road to No. 1*, p. 114.
29	"All that about [Fox] being . . . That's why he's out there.: *The Road to No. 1*, p. 114.
29	I was praying before the . . . a few plays and help the team.: *The Road to No. 1*, p. 114.
30	After Jacoby's freshman season, . . . were falling down.: Snook, *What It Means to Be a Buckeye*, p. 48.
30	Jacoby replied that he . . . but we got him signed.": Snook, *What It Means to Be a Buckeye*, p. 49.
30	After Jacoby graduated and . . . are you doing here?" Snook, *What It Means to Be a Buckeye*, p. 50.
30	Thoroughly amused, Annie . . . pregnant Nina Jacoby.: Snook, *What It Means to Be a Buckeye*, p. 51.
30	Coach would tell our boys . . . get a good education.: Snook, *What It Means to Be a Buckeye*, p. 51.
31	Nobody saw this coming.": Michael Arace, "That's What You Call a Bombshell," *The Columbus Dispatch*, March 5, 2012, http://www.buckeyextra.com/content/stories/2012/03/05.
31	"by all appearances, [they] were fading.": Arace, "That's What You Call a Bombshell."

204

31   Thad Matta acknowledged that . . . on the outside thought.": Bob Baptist, "Buford's Jumper with a Second Left Lifts Buckeyes," *The Columbus Dispatch*, March 5, 2012, http://www.buckeyextra.com/content/stories/2012/03/05/a-title-shot.html.

31   An irate and frustrated Matta even . . . could win the finale.": Arace, "That's What You Call a Bombshell."

31   The place was so noisy . . . to fellow guard William Buford,: Arace, "That's What You Call a Bombshell."

31   Through it all, I've seen this team continue to fight.: Baptist, "Buford's Jumper with a Second Left Lifts Buckeyes."

32   he "holds a status akin to a living folk hero.": "Archie Griffin," *Wikipedia, the free encyclopedia*, http://en.wikipedia.org/wiki/Archie_Griffin.

32   started his football career on . . . Griffin volunteered to step in.: Rapp. p. 102.

32   When Griffin visited the OSU . . . other things, mostly my academics.": Rapp. p. 103.

32   "Son," he said, "you go play football for that man.": Rapp. p. 104.

33   All that stood between the 1968 . . . season and [a] national championship": Menzer, p. 76.

33   duplicating the California heat . . . up to 90 degrees.: Menzer, p. 77.

33   the quarterbacks should hit the . . . Kern was first in line.: Mark Rea, "Rex Kern: Great Guy, Great Stories," *Rea's Day Blog*, June 7, 2008, http://markrea.wordpress.com/2008/06/07/rex-kern-great-guy-great-stories.

33   "Why Rex Kern was not . . . is a question often asked.": Snypp and Hunter, p. 221.

33   So Kern hit the tackling dummy . . . limited motion in that arm.: Rea, "Rex Kern."

34   Tressel attended the Buckeye . . . in Ann Arbor, Michigan.": Menzer, pp. 265-66.

34   Wide receiver Drew Carter and . . . to back that statement up.: Menzer, p. 267.

34   From the day Tressel was hired, . . . of the loss in 2000.: Menzer, p. 269.

34   "I am so proud of these kids,": Menzer, p. 272.

34   I didn't promise this win. I promised you would be proud of us.: Menzer, p. 272.

35   The new coach's relationship with . . . and pay the players myself!": Menzer, p. 38.

35   "and the downtown folks backed off a little.": Menzer, p. 39.

35   after the Michigan game, an older . . . once in his life -- speechless.: Menzer, p. 39.

35   Every day as a person, . . . Which do you want to be?: Snook, *Then Tress Said to Troy . . .*", p. 84.

36   He once memorized the first . . . arranged in alphabetical order.: Alexander Wolff, "Thanks for the Memory," *Sports Illustrated*, June 30, 2003, http://sportsillustrated.cnn.com/vault/article/magazine/MAG1029059/index.htm.

36   his belief that through . . . God was speaking to me.": Wolff, "Thanks for the Memory."

36   You can't study and . . . in there are life-changing.": Wolff, "Thanks for the Memory."

37   I've been thinking about Michigan . . . for a whole year.": Emmanuel, p. 97.

37   the Buckeyes "were being hailed . . . They were a juggernaut": Emmanuel, p. 90.

37   "one of the greatest upsets of all time.": Emmanuel, p. 95.

37   that loss infuriated Woody Hayes. . . . his obsession on to his players.: Emmanuel, p. 97.

37   In the Thursday practice . . . to see if you're ready,": Emmanuel, pp. 97-98.

37   The "biggest revenge game in Ohio State history": Kaelin, p. 84.

37   the largest crowd in Ohio Stadium history.: Kaelin, p. 86.

37   Going to the Rose Bowl wasn't . . . avenging last year's loss.: Emmanuel, p. 98.

38   In 2001, when All-American . . . "Who's Krenzel?": *The Road to No. 1*, p. 80.

38   Krenzel had the "ability to . . . to think on his feet.: *The Road to No. 1*, p. 80.

38   "meld his academic and [his] athletic prowess": The Road to No. 1, p. 80.

38   Krenzel was using a no-huddle offense.: *The Road to No. 1*, p. 56.

38   I just live my life . . . something is wrong or right.: *The Road to No. 1*, p. 80.

39   "Woody Hayes and I . . . threw five interceptions.: Snook, *What It Means to Be a Buckeye*, p. 60.

39   At the one practice after . . . are we going to do?": Snook, *What It Means to Be a Buckeye*, p. 61.

39   the frantic coach hit himself . . . "I don't want to.": Snook, *What It Means to Be a Buckeye*, p. 62.

39   Matte admitted later on . . . really good friends.": Snook, *What It Means to Be a Buckeye*, p. 63.

39   I had never played . . . want to play quarterback.: Snook, *What It Means to Be a Buckeye*, p. 60.

40   Carter "routinely made . . . left teammates agape in practice.": Menzer, p. 205.

40   he was chased out of the pocket . . . Karsatos still didn't believe it.: Menzer, p. 206.

40   Carter snared the ball left-handed . . . that he actually levitated.": Menzer, pp. 206-07.

40   When I saw it on film, it just blew me away.: Menzer, p. 207.

41   "one of the ugliest scenes in the history of sports.": "40 Years Later: Ohio State-Minnesota Brawl," *lostlettermen.com*, http://www.lostlettermen.com/2-14-2012.

41   Minnesota led 32-30 with 11:41 . . . declared the game to be over.: William F. Reed, "An Ugly Affair in Minneapolis," *Sports Illustrated*, Feb. 7, 1972, http://sportsillustrated.cnn.com/vault/article/magazine/MAG1085766.

41 Three Ohio State players were taken . . . 29 stitches to repair the damage.: "Luke Witte," *Wikipedia, the free encyclopedia,* http://en.wikipedia.org/wiki/Luke_Witte.
41 Gopher fans had booed him . . . semiconscious from the floor.": Reed, "An Ugly Affair."
41 It was an ugly, cowardly display of violence.: Reed, "An Ugly Affair."
42 Francis Aloysius Schmidt was quite correctly labeled an "offensive genius.": Menzer, p. 31.
42 Though he was an unknown . . . quickly won Ohio State fans over.: Menzer, p. 29.
42 the first Ohio State coach to use . . . out of any formation,: Menzer, p. 29.
42 even teaching his players not . . . were about to be tackled.: Menzer, p. 30.
42 He had his quarterbacks paste . . . they could remember the offense.: Snypp and Hunter, p. 86.
42 "They put their pants on . . . or whatever he had on hand.: Snypp and Hunter, p. 86.
42 He once was so caught up . . . his car door and stepped out.: Mezner, p. 30.
42 Tradition differs as to whether . . . coach from serious injury.: Both Mezner, p. 30, and Snypp and Hunter, p. 86, tell this story but differ as to whether Schmidt fell all the way to the ground.
43 who didn't particularly like . . . found out who did it.": Snook, *Then Tress Said to Troy . . .",* p. 215.
44 The running back/defensive back . . . I have ever seen": Snypp and Hunter, p. 163.
44 Sportswriters said he "hopped all . . . fictional character Hopalong Cassidy.: "Howard Cassady," *Wikipedia, the free encyclopedia,* http://en.wikipedia.org/wiki/Howard_Cassady.
44 never had a pass completed on him.: "Howard Cassady."
44 in 1953 when he was . . . "You're hitting the line too fast.": "Howard Cassady."
44 In the mid-1980s while . . . and returned to its owner.: Mark Schlabach, "Buckeye Bronze, 1955 Heisman Winner Howard Cassady," *The Heisman 75 Years,* http://espn.go.com/ncf/features/heisman/_/year/1955/set/3.
44 The price of silver was way up . . . value of the Heisman.: Schlabach, "Buckeye Bronze, 1955."
45 Marder was in high school . . . off the center-field wall.: Jeremy McLaughlin, "Power Source," *The Columbus Dispatch,* May 14, 2010, http://www.dispatch.com/content/stories/sports/2010/05/14/power-source.html.
45 She hit seven home runs in her first 48 at-bats: McLaughlin, "Power Source."
45 It's a good thing we got there early enough to watch her warm up.: McLaughlin, "Power Source."
46 Eddie was 15 years old when . . . but he caught on.: Menzer, p. 240.
46 "His size and strength . . . attitude toward authority figures softened.": Menzer, p. 241.
46 He dropped his head into his hands, . . . his last hug for his mother.: Menzer, p. 244.
46 I was hardheaded, and I didn't . . . my mom had to send me away.: Menzer, 240.
47 "The strangest thing happened . . . OSU locker room.: Snook, *Then Tress Said to Troy . . .",* p. 27.
47 He rushed for 108 yards against his alma mater in that 1942 game.: Snook, *Then Tress Said to Troy . . .",* p. 27.
47 "I still cherish the pair of gold . . . who were national champions.": Snook, *Then Tress Said to Troy . . .",* p. 28.
47 Here I was, playing my alma --- was awful strange to me.: Snook, *Then Tress Said to Troy . . .",* p. 27.
48 he spent four injury-plagued . . . I knew he could kick,": Robert Gartrell, "Barclay Takes Different Route to Kicking Stardom," *The Lantern,* Oct. 21, 2010, http://www.thelantern.com/sports.
48 "from complete obscurity into Buckeye lore.": Gartrell, "Barclay Takes Different Route ."
48 Barclay was the oldest player on a major college team.: Steven Goff, "Ohio State Buckeyes Kicker Devin Barclay," *Washington Post,* March 29, 2011, http://www.washingtonpost.com/blogs/soccer-insider/post.
48 It just helped me grow up . . . the patterns of success.: Gartrell, "Barclay Takes Different Route."
49 Senn played with a passion . . . it might be bad,": Mechelle Voepel, "Ohio State Still Honoring Connor Senn," *ESPN.com,* Sept. 26, 2011, http://espn.go.com/college-sports/story/_/id/7023028.
49 The shattered Buckeye team . . . the story about Connor,": Voepel, "Ohio State Still Honoring Connor Senn."
49 I think he'd be happy. . . . his memory and his tradition.: Voepel, "Ohio State Still Honoring Connor Senn."
50 "Perhaps no other player was . . . if not his favorite.": Snook, *Then Tress Said to Troy . . .",* p. 89.
50 Offensive tackle Dave Cheney, who . . . about Woody being his father.": Snook, *Then Tress Said to Troy . . .",* p. 90.
50 Hayes asked the freshman . . . on this small country road,": Snook, *Then Tress Said to Troy . . .",* p. 91.
50 "We ended up in the same . . . lets Woody drive them!": Snook, *Then Tress Said to Troy . . .",* p. 92.
52 "Let's face it: The only . . . 13 tries against the Wolverines.": Austin Murphy, "Perfect Ending," *Sports Illustrated Presents Ohio State Buckeyes* (New York City: Time Inc., 2003), p. 45.
52 inserted especially for this game.: Austin Murphy, "Perfect Ending," p. 42.
53 Jared Sullinger said a Badger . . . as the game wore on.: "No. 1 Ohio State Breaks 3s Record," *ncaa.com,* March 6, 2011, http://ncaa.com/news/basketball-men/2011-03-06.

53   "The rest of the game . . . raise the Big Ten trophy.: "No. 1 Ohio State Breaks 3s Record."
54   "a really sweet team . . . "Why not 28 or 35?": Doug Lesmerises, "Gone in 88 Seconds," *The Plain Dealer*, Sept. 16, 2007.
54   "They were stumbling, . . . just going and going and going,": Lesmerises, "Gone in 88 Seconds."
54   It was pretty funny how it worked out.: Lesmerises, "Gone in 88 Seconds."
55   Amling wasn't recruited out of . . . we were the civilian champs.": Snook, *What It Means to Be a Buckeye*, p. 10.
55   Head coach Carroll Widdoes . . . "Neither.": Snook, *What It Means to Be a Buckeye*, p. 11.
55   Thank goodness, Coach was an understanding man.: Snook, *What It Means to Be a Buckeye*, p. 11.
56   In 1972, Hayes and assistant . . . a few drops in that tank.": Snook, *Then Tress Said to Troy . . .*", p. 165.
56   Center Jim Conroy related the . . . without him saying it,": Snook, *Then Tress Said to Troy . . .*", p. 166.
56   Linebacker Randy Gradishar tells . . . crowd went wild.": Snook, *Then Tress Said to Troy . . .*", p. 166.
56   It is true that Woody . . . I was a witness to it.": Snook, *Then Tress Said to Troy . . .*", p. 165.
57   Fathalikhani came to Columbus . . . to be a starting catcher.": Alex Kopilow, "Plate to Mound," *The Lantern*, May 4, 2011, http://www.thelantern.com/sports/plate-to-mound.
57   Sometime before the start . . . just for the fun of it.: Kopilow, "Plate to Mound."
57   Pete Jenkins liked what . . . to help this team,": Mark Znidar, "Ex-Catcher Pitches in as Reliever," *The Columbus Dispatch*, April 15, 2011, http://www.dispatch.com/content/stories/sports/2011/04/15.
57   I'm not content with the success I have had so far.: Kopilow, "Plate to Mound."
58   What more can I say, man?": Doug Lesmerises, "One Title Down, Another Title to Go," *The Plain Dealer*, Nov. 19, 2006, p. W5.
58   "turned his Big Ten hat . . . Jim Tressel and smiled,": Lesmerises, "One Title Down."
58   "a fast-break game" and "Smith ran the anchor leg.": Lesmerises, "One Title Down."
59   Tom Cousineau believes he . . . see Woody Hayes alive.: Snook, *What It Means to Be a Buckeye*, p. 162.
59   "It looked like a small . . . firing until he landed.: Snook, *What It Means to Be a Buckeye*, p. 161.
59   "In the end, I loved . . . "Well, he died today.": Snook, *What It Means to Be a Buckeye*, p. 162.
60   "Woody must have worked . . . out to win the first one.": Snypp and Hunter, p. 147.
60   Hayes later said he was afraid . . . working on a one-year contract.": Snypp and Hunter, p. 148.
60   During the 16-14 win over . . . He never did.: Snook, *Then Tress Said to Troy . . .*", p. 39.
60   The worst blowup I saw . . . off the hinges to get in.: Snook, *Then Tress Said to Troy . . .*", p. 39.
61   Legend has it that Woody . . . Why play them?": Snook, *Then Tress Said to Troy . . .*", p. 123.
61   He fell face-first leading . . . as fast as I used to be.": Snook, *Then Tress Said to Troy . . .*", p. 123.
61   They made the mistakes and we capitalized.: *Greatest Moments in Ohio State Football History*, p. 166.
62   It's out hot out here, . . . inside of Ty Tucker's sweatpants.": Tom Reed, "Tennis Transformer," *The Plain Dealer*, May 13, 2010, http://www.dispatch.com/content/stories/sports/2010/05/13/tennis-transformer.html.
62   for months after the 2009 . . . want to look at it.": Reed, "Tennis Transformer."
62   the second-most "distinctive . . . and his match-day socks.: Reed, "Tennis Transformer."
62   Let's just say we've all got to do what makes us feel comfortable.: Reed, "Tennis Transformer."
63   "It was as if he had . . . may be at any specific time.": Snook, *Then Tress Said to Troy . . .*", p. 54.
63   A friend of Schumacher's who . . . was committing to OSU.: Snook, *Then Tress Said to Troy . . .*", p. 54.
63   Hayes then invited the . . . signee sealing the deal.: Snook, *Then Tress Said to Troy . . .*", pp. 54-55.
63   I never asked [Hayes] . . . I'll probably never know.: Snook, *Then Tress Said to Troy . . .*", p. 55.
64   Late in the summer before. . . before their next game.: Snook, *What It Means to Be a Buckeye*, p. 331.
64   "This is big, this is big, . . . him couldn't block him.": Snook, *What It Means to Be a Buckeye*, p. 334.
64   "the most important quarterback pressure in Ohio State history.": Snook, *What It Means to Be a Buckeye*, p. 335.
64   "I got the best jump . . . know what had happened.": Snook, *What It Means to Be a Buckeye*, p. 334.
64   "a homely pass [that] fluttered to the turf.: Austin Murphy, "Flat-Out Fantastic," *Sports Illustrated Presents Ohio State Buckeyes* (New York City: Time Inc., 2003), p. 54.
64   A few weeks later, on . . . of that magical season.: Snook, *What It Means to Be a Buckeye*, p. 335.
64   It was cold . . . I am glad I did it.: Snook, *What It Means to Be a Buckeye*, p. 335.
65   In the fall of 1943, . . . after he arrived in Columbus.: Snook, *What It Means to Be a Buckeye*, p. 28.
65   "The team was a bunch of . . . was in the war.": Snook, *What It Means to Be a Buckeye*, p. 28.
65   Only five of the squad's 44 . . . surgery for varicose veins.: Jack Park, *The Official Ohio State Football Encyclopedia* (Champaign, IL: Sports Publishing LLC, 2003), p. 208.
65   Not a single player weighed . . . 44 guys on the team,: Park, p. 209.
65   flying 26 missions during . . . out for the team.: Snook, *What It Means to Be a Buckeye*, p. 29.

65   I was just a young kid lost in the big city.: Snook, *What It Means to Be a Buckeye*, p. 28.

66   It was a moment that had seemed impossible.": Doug Lesmerises, "An OSU Block Party," *The Plain Dealer*, March 23, 2007.

66   "with more speed and . . . in the first place.": Lesmerises, "An OSU Block Party."

66   No team in the history . . . to win in regulation.: "Oden Blocks Smith's Last Effort," *ESPN.com*, March 22, 2007, http://espn.go.com/ncb/recap?gameId=274000038.

66   We knew if we took . . . There was a lot of time.: "Oden Blocks Smith's Last Effort."

67   Ecstatic Buckeye fans tore up . . . some players onto their shoulders.: Rapp, pp. 132-33.

67   "People like to say they're . . . I was nervous the whole game.": Rapp, p. 132.

67   Elated Buckeye fans partied . . . near one end zone to get there.: Rapp, pp. 132-33.

67   When he met reporters after . . . he had received from his wife.: Rapp, p. 133.

67   We'll pay for it.: Rapp, p. 133.

68   His sophomore season Cordle . . . list after switching positions.: Ken Gordon, "Ohio State's Cordle Wants Look from NFL," *The Columbus Dispatch*, Jan. 22. 2010, http://www.dispatch.com/content/stories/sports/2010/01/22/osufb_all-stars.ART.

68   in 2007 when he injured . . . with his other hand.": Doug Lesmerises,. "Left of Center, Cordle Still on Target," *The Plain Dealer*, Oct. 20, 2007.

68   When the 2009 season ended, . . . the East-West Shrine Game.: Gordon, "Ohio State's Cordle."

68   I know I'm not the . . . you at least get a look.: Gordon, "Ohio State's Cordle."

69   All-American tackle Dave Foley had . . . don't throw an interception!": Menzer, p. 73.

69   the wily coach knew that Purdue's . . . and we never huddle.": Menzer, p. 71.

69   "I've got spit hanging out . . . don't throw an interception!": Menzer, p. 73.

69   dragging two defenders across the goal line: Menzer, p. 73.

69   "Suddenly, the Buckeyes were beginning . . . the best team in the nation.": Menzer, p. 74.

69   This is great, man. Way to listen to me, Billy.: Menzer, p. 73.

70   "the noisiest and most . . . building in the Big Ten.": Jim Massie, "Lavender Sets Mark in Victory," *The Columbus Dispatch*, Feb. 14, 2011, http://www.dispatch.com/content/stories/sports/ 2011/02/14/lavender-sets-mark-in-victory.html.

70   "the death-grip state of a sizzling second half,": Massie, "Lavender Sets Mark."

70   I didn't know. . . . on my mind and just play.: Massie, "Lavender Sets Mark."

71   "reached a level that . . . era's Cold War participants shiver.": Emmanuel, p. 99.

71   to raise "the football drama from . . . that model for his team.: Emmanuel, p. 99.

71   On a trip to Ann Arbor, . . . distract his team from the game.: Emmanuel, p. 99.

71   There aren't any secrets in coaching.: Bettinger, p. 31.

72   "If he gets stitches can he go back in? Will it be a problem?": *The Road to No. 1*, p. 32.

72   it was bleeding around the incision.: *The Road to No. 1*, p. 32.

72   All of us in the stadium . . . We're better when he's playing.: *The Road to No. 1*, p. 32.

73   One of the most significant single plays during Woody Hayes' 28 seasons": Park, p. 294.

73   After being told by his coach . . . by the Michigan game.: Park, p. 294.

74   The Buckeye coaches had . . . collect at another spot.: Snook, *What It Means to Be a Buckeye*, p. 177.

74   no one had told him where he would be playing.: Snook, *What It Means to Be a Buckeye*, pp. 177-78.

74   So Fox asked assistant . . . So he joined Cassady: Snook, *What It Means to Be a Buckeye*, p. 178.

74   On that picture day, jerseys . . . "That dampened my enthusiasm,": Snook, *What It Means to Be a Buckeye*, p. 177.

75   "arguably the most prominent . . . network for college football.": Matt Hinton, "'Relentless' Buckeye Fans Have Driven Kirk Herbstreit from Ohio," *Dr. Saturday*, March 12, 2011, http://rivals.yahoo.com/ncaa/football/blog/dr_satuday/post.

75   He usually has his own . . . feel like they know him.": Mary Schmitt Boyer, "Shy TV Host Masters Bright Lights," *The Plain Dealer*, Nov. 4, 2007, p. C1.

75   "When they hired me . . . 'Who is this guy?'": Boyer, "Shy TV Host Masters Bright Lights."

75   Everywhere he goes, . . . to be like him.: Boyer, "Shy TV Host Masters Bright Lights."

76   but noticed a weird and recurring . . . to come visit the campus.: Larry Watts, "Walking Before She Runs," *BigTen.org*, Oct. 23, 2010, http://www.bigten.org/sports/w-xc/spec-rel/102310aaa.html.

76   one of the squad's top four runners.: Watts, "Walking Before She Runs."

76   "anything is possible . . . willing to work hard.": Watts, "Walking Before She Runs."

76   I've learned a lot . . . how much I love running.: Watts, "Walking Before She Runs."

77   Hayes was well known "for . . .and never said a word.: Snook, *Then Tress Said to Troy . . .*", p. 219.

78   He was careful to take . . . as a Buckeye was over.: Snook, *What It Means to Be a Buckeye*, p. 339.

78   Weeks later, at the celebration . . . so much of my life.: Snook, *What It Means to Be a Buckeye*, p. 339.

78   Just moments before the team . . . team helmet to the president.: Snook, *What It Means to Be a Buckeye*, p. 339.

78   I just sat down . . . we had done was special.: Snook, *What It Means to Be a Buckeye*, p. 339.

79   From the spring of 2008 . . . the spring and the summer.: Doug Lesmerises, "Buckeyes Star Turner Reached the Summit," *The Plain Dealer*, March 8, 2010.

79   "My first two or three . . . "This is how you do it,": Lesmerises, "Buckeyes Star Turner."

79   When a lot of players . . . It was like therapy to me.: Lesmerises, "Buckeyes Star Turner."

80   When the final horn sounded, . . . the whistle for the last play.: Snypp and Hunter, p. 104.

80   Stungis had never attempted a place kick before. Snypp and Hunter, p. 104.

80   Many of the spectators who had . . . that the Buckeys had won: Snypp and Hunter, p. 104.

80   Most of us had taken our . . . It was amazing.: Snook, *Then Tress Said to Troy . . .*", p. 32.

81   In the winter of 1979, . ., told you I would do it.": Snook, *Then Tress Said to Troy . . .*", p. 104.

81   Bruce simply smiled in reply,: Snook, *Then Tress Said to Troy . . .*", p. 105.

82   after hearing the great Red . . . to his players that afternoon.: Menzer, p. 54.

82   had his excitement turn to frustration . . . was only blank stares.: Menzer, p. 54.

82   "How can they not know . . . he waited for the big moment.": Menzer, p. 54.

82   The Ghost and his entourage did make . . . and left for the airport.: Menzer, p. 55.

83   Matt Sylvester had dreamed . . . he wasn't fantasizing.: Bruce Hooley, "Dream Rises to Top," *The Plain Dealer*, March 7, 2005.

83   Almost six years after the . . . in his time in Columbus.: Doug Lesmerises, "OSU-Illini Game in '05 Turned Schools' Programs," *The Plain Dealer*, Jan. 22, 2011.

83   who openly talked about . . . literally said those words.": Hooley, "Dream Rises to Top."

83   drew a play up for . . . I'm going to make it,": Hooley, "Dream Rises to Top."

83   I feel like I'm going to . . . all going to be over.: Hooley, "Dream Rises to Top."

84   In 1974 Woody Hayes assembled evidence . . . on them to the NCAA.: Menzer, p. 122.

84   "The referee called a touchdown, . . . hallway to the Spartan locker room.: Menzer, p. 123.

84   Hayes flung open an outer door . . . "Guys, we're going home.": Menzer, p. 124.

84   Run 'em over!: Menzer, p. 124.

85   the powers that be generally . . . to offer George a scholarship.: Austin Murphy, "So You Wanna Play on Sunday?" *Sports Illustrated Presents Ohio State Buckeyes* (New York City: Time Inc., 2003), p. 71.

86   Jim Tressel practically begged . . . tribute to him in particular.: Robert Gartrell, "The Man Behind the Uniform," *The Lantern*, Nov. 22, 2010, http://www.thelantern.com/sports.

86   he was the smallest tackle in the conference.: Gartrell, "The Man Behind the Uniform."

86   He was drafted into the . . . of your being killed.": Gartrell, "The Man Behind the Uniform."

86   It's one of those things . . . since forgotten about it.: Gartrell, "The Man Behind the Uniform."

87   One year, Bailey sought . . . Nobody cared.: Judith Ball Fountain, "Abstract: Phyllis J. Bailey Interview," *Knowledge Bank: The Ohio State University*, https://kb.osu.edu/dspace/handle/1811/29293?mode=full.

87   She had tryouts and thus began . . . the women play in St. John.: Katie Logan, "Women's Basketball Celebrates 40 years of Memories," *The Lantern*, March 10, 2005, http://www.thelantern.com/2.1351.

87   Bailey's early teams also battled . . . locker or training rooms.: Fountain, "Abstract."

87   At Ohio State early in the 20th . . . allowed to watch them play.: Fountain, "Abstract."

88   "was a real character who loved to have a good time.": Snook, *Then Tress Said to Troy . . .*", p. 209.

88   on Christmas Day 1968 as . . . not to cross the border.: Snook, *Then Tress Said to Troy . . .*", p. 209.

88   The group conned starting . . . sneak into his hotel room.: Snook, *Then Tress Said to Troy . . .*", p. 210.

88   As the clock ran down, . . . to go into this game.": Snook, *Then Tress Said to Troy . . .*", p. 211.

88   He opened up his parka to reveal that he didn't have a helmet or a jersey.: Snook, *Then Tress Said to Troy . . .*", p. 212.

88   Rusnak had decided that he . . . She did: Snook, *Then Tress Said to Troy . . .*", p. 211.

89   "certainly a quality win for us.": *The Road to No. 1*, p. 44.

89   "I was catching that with . . . there was a baby in there.": *The Road to No. 1*, p. 44.

89   A trend had developed of . . . at midfield and knelt in prayer.: *The Road to No. 1*, p. 44.

90   In five-degree weather, snow . . . up to 40 miles per hour.: Snypp and Hunter, p. 132.

90   The game was late starting . . . had frozen to the field it covered.: Snypp and Hunter, pp. 132-33.

90   When junior guard Thor Ronemus . . . a snowstorm like that.": Snook, *Then Tress Said to Troy . . .*", p. 37.

90   He remembered that many of the . . . coming down a water slide.": Snook, *Then Tress Said to Troy . . .*", p. 38.

90   Michigan didn't complete a pass . . . and punted 45 times.: Snypp and Hunter, p. 135.

90   "With wind, snow, sleet, and hands as handicaps,": Snypp and Hunter, p. 134.

90   The ball "went up on a . . . It just disappeared.": Snook, *Then Tress Said to Troy . . .*", p. 37.

90   With forty seconds left in the first half,: Snook, *Then Tress Said to Troy . . .*", p. 38.
90   "brought Fesler to a temporary state of depression": Snook, *Then Tress Said to Troy . . .*", p. 38.
90   It was a nightmare. . . . It was terrible out there.: Snook, *Then Tress Said to Troy . . .*", p. 38.
91   In the eighth grade, DeLeone . . . kitchen of their apartment.: Snook, *What It Means to Be a Buckeye*, p. 163.
91   DeLeone arrived in Columbus . . . may as well hang around.: Snook, *What It Means to Be a Buckeye*, p. 164.
92   The first time anyone clocked . . . to increase his speed.: Bill Livingston, "Holding Fast to Principles," *The Plain Dealer*, Jan. 7, 2007.
92   he was recruited to Ohio . . . track career on hold.: "Ted Ginn, Jr.", *Wikipedia, the free encyclopedia*, http://en.wikipedia.org/wiki/Ted_Ginn,_Jr.
92   clocked at 4.28 in the 40. He said his best time was 4.22.: "Ted Ginn, Jr.," *Wikipedia*.
92   I wasn't born fast.; Livingston, "Holding Fast to Principles."
93   "I think people thought I . . . were myself and Greg Oden,": Doug Lesmerises, "Big Lift," *The Plain Dealer*, Jan. 24, 2007.
93   Matta finally threatened to . . . start shooting more often.: Lesmerises "Big Lift."
93   telling Oden he felt like he would get the ball and make the shot.: Doug Lesmerises, "Victory an Ugly Beauty," *The Plain Dealer*, Feb. 26, 2007.
93   The guy that gets overshadowed . . . such a super talent.: Lesmerises, "Big Lift."
94   Only a day after a . . . "Yeah, sure, of course.": Snook, *What It Means to Be a Buckeye*, p. 237.
94   "I hadn't talked to . . . new outlook on things.: Snook, *What It Means to Be a Buckeye*, p. 239.
95   One Friday that year President . . . back to the Buckeye quarterback.: Snook, *What It Means to Be a Buckeye*, p. 317.
96   a "stale exchange of punts" . . . able to catch me.": Doug Lesmerises, "Big Returns with Big Dividends Pay Off," *The Plain Dealer*, Oct. 11, 2009, p. C1.
96   "I got a couple of . . . and that was all,": Lesmerises, "Big Returns with Big Dividends."
96   "I was surprised they kicked it to me,": Livingston, " Tomorrow Is Finally Today," *The Plain Dealer*, Oct. 11, 2009, p. C1.
96   He "burst out of the . . . seen at Ohio State: Livingston, " Tomorrow Is Finally Today."
96   "He looked like he was shot out of a gun,": Livingston, " Tomorrow Is Finally Today."
96   none of which ran off the game clock: Livingston, " Tomorrow Is Finally Today."
96   He took that thing . . . and he was gone.: Livingston, " Tomorrow Is Finally Today."
97   "He's a better young man than . . . the best football player I've ever seen.": Menzer, p. 125.
97   Before his senior season even began, . . . think about it all the time.": Menzer, p. 126.
97   He recalled Hayes' admonition that . . . then receive it as a gift.: Menzer, p. 127.
97   When I read that verse, . . . a big weight off my shoulders.: Menzer, p. 127.
98   Syracuse University, only a few . . . out of high school.: Patrick Maks, "OSU Wrestling Coach Tom Ryan Pushes for Success," *The Lantern*, March 8, 2012, http://www.thelantern.com/sports.
98   Ryan's heart, though, was . . . "there's no looking back.": Maks, "OSU Wrestling Coach Tom Ryan Pushes for Success."
98   I had this ache inside . . . was to go [to the University of Iowa]. "OSU Wrestling Coach Tom Ryan Pushes for Success."
99   "perhaps no Ohio State team than the 1987 squad.": Snook, "*Then Tress Said to Troy . . .*", p. 113.
99   Sophomore guard Joe Staysniak . . . can't say anything about that,": "*Then Tress Said to Troy . . .*", Snook, p. 114.
99   Bruce didn't have one of . . . Bruce's display in the Hall.: Snook, "*Then Tress Said to Troy . . .*", p. 114.
99   We thought it was a great idea to honor a wonderful coach and a good man.: Snook, "*Then Tress Said to Troy . . .*", p. 114.
100   He fumbled on his one and only . . . scramble to find his helmet.: Rapp, p. 104.
100   "We weren't running the ball . . . "You guys up North can't block.": Rapp, pp. 104, 106.
100   "You guys from North Carolina can't tackle.": Rapp, p. 106.

BIBLIOGRAPHY

"40 Years Later: Ohio State-Minnesota Brawl." *lostlettermen.com*. http://www.lostlettermen.com/2-14/2012.

Arace, Michael. "That's What You Call a Bombshell." *The Columbus Dispatch*. 5 March 2012. http://www.buckeyextra.com/content/stories/2012/03/05.

"Archie Griffin." *Wikipedia, the free encyclopedia*. htt://en.wikipedia.org/wiki/Archie_Griffin.

Avery, Todd. "Ohio State Pitcher Andrew Armstrong Overcomes 'Death Sentence.'" *The Lantern*. 1 May 2011. http://www.thelantern.com/sports.

Baptist, Bob. "Buford's Jumper with a Second Left Lifts Buckeyes to Share of Big Ten Championship." *The Columbus Dispatch*. 5 March 2012. http://www.buckeyextra.com/content/stories/2012/03/05/a-title-shot.html.

Bettinger, Jim & Julie S. *The Book of Bowden*. Nashville: TowleHouse Publishing, 2001.

Boyer, Mary Schmitt. "Shy TV Host Masters Bright Lights." *The Plain Dealer*. 4 Nov. 2007. C1.

Emmanuel, Greg. *The 100-Yard War: Inside the 100-Year-Old Michigan-Ohio State Football Rivalry*. Hoboken, N.J.: John Wiley & Sons, 2004.

Finney, Peter, Jr. "Terrelle Pryor, Buckeyes' Defense Shines in Sugar Bowl Victory over Arkansas." *aolnews.com*. 5 Jan. 2011. http://www.aolnews.com/2011/01/05.

Fountain, Judith Ball. "Abstract: Phyllis J. Bailey Interview." *Knowledge Bank: The Ohio State University*. https://kb.osu.edu/dspace/hadnle/1811/29293?mode=full.

Gartrell, Robert. "Barclay Takes Different Route to Kicking Stardom." *The Lantern*. 21 Oct. 2010. http://www.thelantern.com/sports.

---. "Moeller Hoping to Finally Catch a Break." *The Lantern*. 21 Oct. 2010. http://www.thelantern.com/sports.

---. "The Man Behind the Uniform." *The Lantern*. 22 Nov. 2010. http://www.thelantern.com/sports.

Goff, Steven. "Ohio State Buckeyes Kicker Devin Barclay Returns to His Soccer Roots." *Washington Post*. 29 March 2011. http://www.washingtonpost.com/blogs/soccer-insider/post.

Gordon, Ken. "Ohio State's Cordle Wants Look from NFL." *The Columbus Dispatch*. 22 Jan. 2010. http://www.dispatch.com/content/stories/sports/2010/01/22/osufb_all-stars.ART.

Greatest Moments in Ohio State Football History. Chicago: Triumph Books, 2003.

Hays, Graham. "OSU's Pruner Finds Peace After Tragedy." *ESPN.com*. 16 April 2009.http://sports.espn.go.com/ncaa/columns/story?columnist=hays_graham&id=4073311.

Hinton, Matt. "'Relentless' Buckeye Fans Have Driven Kirk Herbstreit from Ohio." *Dr. Saturday*. 12 March 2011. http://rivals.yahoo.com/ncaa/football/blog/drsaturday/post.

Hooley, Bruce. "Dream Rises to Top: Buckeyes Hand Illini First Loss." *The Plain Dealer*. 7 March 2005.

"Howard Cassady." *Wikipedia, the free encyclopedia*. http://en.wikipedia.org/wiki/Howard_Cassady.

Kaelin, Eric. *Buckeye Glory Days: The Most Memorable Games of Ohio State Football*. Champaign, IL: Sports Publishing L.L.C., 2004.

King, Kelley. "Senior Moment." *Sports Illustrated Presents Ohio State Buckeyes*. New York City: Time Inc., 2003. 46-49.

Kopilow, Alex. "Plate to Mound: New Role for Buckeye Catcher-Turned Pitcher David Fathalikhani." *The Lantern*. 4 May 2011. http://www.thelantern.com/sports/plate-to-mound.

Lesmerises, Doug. "An OSU Block Party: Oden's Defense Stops Tennessee on Final Shot." *The Plain Dealer*. 23 March 2007.

---. "Big Lift." *The Plain Dealer*. Jan. 24, 2007.

---. "Big Returns with Big Dividends Pay Off in Victory for Buckeyes." *The Plain Dealer*. 11 Oct. 2009. C1.

---. "Buckeyes are Happy Campers." *The Plain Dealer*. 5 Oct. 2008.

---. "Buckeyes Star Turner Reached the Summit on Sweat, Hard Work." *The Plain Dealer*. 8 March 2010.

---. "Gone in 88 Seconds: Buckeyes Take Off in Third Quarter." *The Plain Dealer*. 16 Sept. 2007.

---. "Left of Center, Cordle Still on Target." *The Plain Dealer*. 20 Oct. 2007.

---. "One Title Down, Another Title to Go." *The Plain Dealer*. 19 Nov. 2006. W5.

---. "OSU-Illini Game in '05 Turned Schools' Programs." *The Plain Dealer*. 22 Jan. 2011.

---. "Victory an Ugly Beauty; Oden, Lewis Help Secure Narrow Win." *The Plain Dealer*. 26 Feb. 2007. C1.

Livingston, Bill. "Holding Fast to Principles: Swift-Footed Receiver Ted Ginn Jr. Is a Big-Time Talent." *The Plain Dealer*. 7 Jan. 2007.

---. "Pryor Finishes on Stage with Panache." *The Plain Dealer*. 5 Oct. 2008.

---. "Tomorrow Is Finally Today as OSU's Small Comes Up Big." *The Plain Dealer*. 11 Oct. 2009. C1.

Logan, Katie. "Women's Basketball Celebrates 40 Years of Memories." *The Lantern*. 10 March 2005. http://www.thelantern.com/2.1351.

"Luke Witte." *Wikipedia, the free encyclopedia*. http://en.wikipedia.org/wiki/Luke_Witte.

MacArthur, John. *Twelve Ordinary Men*. Nashville: W Publishing Group, 2002.

Maks, Patrick. "OSU Wrrestling Coach Tom Ryan Pushes for Success On, Off the Mat." *The Lantern*. 8 March 2012. http://www.thelantern.com/sports.

Massie, Jim. "Lavender Sets Mark in Victory." *The Columbus Dispatch*. 14 Feb. 2011. http://www.dispatch. com/content/stories/sports/2011/02/14/lavender-sets-mark-in-victory.html.

---. "Unstoppable: Samantha Prahalis Learned Her Game by Knocking Heads with the Players." *The Columbus Dispatch*. 16 March 2010. http://www.dispatch.com/content/stories/sports/2010/03/16/ unstoppable.html.

May, Tim. "Season to Remember." *The Columbus Dispatch*. 10 May 2011. http://www.dispatch.com/content/ stories/sports/2011/05/10/season-to-remember.html.

McLaughlin, Jeremy. "Power Source." *The Columbus Dispatch*. 14 May 2010. http://www.dispatch.com/ content/stories/sports/2010/05/14/power-source.html.

Menzer, Joe. *Buckeye Madness: The Glorious, Tumultuous, Behind-the-Scenes Story of Ohio State Football*. New York: Simon & Schuster, 2005.

Murphy, Austin. "Flat-Out Fantastic." *Sports Illustrated Presents Ohio State Buckeyes*. New York City: Time Inc., 2003. 50-58.

---. "Perfect Ending." *Sports Illustrated Presents Ohio State Buckeyes*. New York City: Time Inc., 2003. 38-40, 42, 44-45.

---. "So You Wanna Play on Sunday?" *Sports Illustrated Presents Ohio State Buckeyes*. New York City: Time Inc., 2003. 66-71.

"No. 1 Ohio State Breaks 3s Record." *ncaa.com*. 6 March 2011. http://ncaa.com/news/basketball-men/ 2011-03-06.

"The One and Only Jesse Owens Is Big Ten Icon No. 3. *ohiostatebuckeyes.com*. 14 Feb. 2011. http://www. ohiostatebuckeyes.com/genrel/021811aaa.html.

"Oden Blocks Smith's Last Effort: Buckeyes Top Vols." *ESPN.com*. 22 March 2007. http://espn.go.com/ncb/ recap?gameId=274000038.

Park, Jack. *The Official Ohio State Football Encyclopedia*. Champaign, IL: Sports Publishing LLC, 2003.

Periatt, Michael. "The 1: Passion Propels Walk-On Eddie Days." *The Lantern*. 4 April 2011. http://www. thelantern.com/sports.

Rapp, Jeff. *Stadium Stories: Ohio State Buckeyes: Colorful Tales of the Scarlet and Gray*. Guilford, CN: The Globe Pequot Press, 2003.

Rea, Mark. "Rex Kern: Great Guy, Great Stories." *Rea's Day Blog*. 7 June 2008. http://markrea.wordpress. com/2008/06/07/rex-kern-great-guy-great-stories.

Reed, Tom. "Tennis Transformer: OSU Went from Laughingstock to Powerhouse Under Superstitious, Hardworking Coach Ty Tucker." *The Plain Dealer*. 13 May 2010. http://www.dispatch.com/content/ stories/sports/2010/05/13/tennis-transformer.html.

Reed, William F. "An Ugly Affair in Minneapolis." *Sports Illustrated*. 7 Feb. 1972. http://sportsillustrated. cnn.com/vault/article/magazine/MAG1085766.

Restivo, Danny. "Prahalis Reflects on 4 Years as a Buckeye After Record-Breaking Performance." *The Lantern*. 23 Feb. 2012. http://www.thelantern.com/sports.

The Road to No. 1: The 2002 Ohio State Buckeyes' National Championship Season. Texas Football/Epic Sports Corp., 2003.

Schlabach, Mark. "Buckeye Bronze, 1955 Heisman Winner Howard Cassady." *The Heisman 75 Years*. http:// espn.co.com/ncf/features/heisman/_/year/1955/set/3.

Snook, Jeff. *"Then Tress Said to Troy . . .": The Best Ohio State Football Stories Ever Told*. Chicago: Triumph Books, 2007.

Snook, Jeff, ed. *What It Means to Be a Buckeye*. Chicago: Triumph Books, 2003.

Snypp, Wilbur. *The Buckeyes: A Story of Ohio State Football*. Huntsville, AL: The Strode Publishers, 1974.

Snypp, Wilbur and Bob Hunter. *The Buckeyes: Ohio State Football*. Tomball, TX: The Strode Publishers, 1988.

"Ted Ginn, Jr." *Wikipedia, the free encylopedia*. http://en.wikipedia.org/wiki/Ted_Ginn,_Jr.

Voepel, Mechelle. "Ohio State Still Honoring Connor Senn." *ESPN.com*. 26 Sept. 2011. http://espn.go.com/ college-sports/story/_/id/7023028.

Watts, Larry. "Kicking Around All Options." *BigTen.org*. 4 Feb. 2011. http://www.bigtenorg/genrel/020411. aaa.html.

---. "Walking Before She Runs." *BigTen.org*. 23 Oct. 2010. http://www.bigten.org/sports/w-xc/spec-rel/ 102310aaa.html.

Wolff, Alexander. "Thanks for the Memory." *Sports Illustrated*. 30 June 2003. http://sportsillustrated.cnn. com/vault/article/magazine/MAG10290592/index.htm.

Znidar, Mark, "Ex-Catcher Pitches in as Reliever." *The Columbus Dispatch*. 15 April 2011. http:// www.dispatch.com/content/stories/sports/2011/04/15.

BUCKEYES

INDEX
(LAST NAME, DEVOTION DAY NUMBER)

Alford, Steve 93
Allen, Will 29, 52
Ames, K.L. 1
Amling, Warren 55
Anderson, Garret 13
Anderson, Tim 89
Armstrong, Andrew 3
Auerbach, Red 95
Bacall, Aaron 33
Bailey, Phyllis 87
Barclay, Devin 48
Barkley, Charles 43
Barry, Rick 88
Barton, Kirk 54
Bartschy, Ross 21
Baschnagel, Brian 11, 74, 84
Bellisari, Steve 34
Bentley, LeCharles 38
Biggs, Ernie 60
Bluem, John 49
Bobo, Hubert 30, 73
Boeckman, Todd 54, 68
Bollman, Jim 68
Bonhaus, Matt 61
Boone, Alex 54
Boston, David 13
Bowden, Bobby 21, 71
Brown, Paul 15, 80
Bruce, Earle 81, 99
Bryant, Bear 4, 58
Buford, William 31
Burkhart, Dan 57
Byars, Keith 46
Carter, Cris 40
Carter, Drew 34
Cassady, Craig 74
Cassady, Howard 44, 58
Cassidy, Hopalong 44
Chaump, George 88
Cheney, Dave 50
Clarett, Maurice 2, 29, 52, 72
Clark, Jimmy 9
Clinton, Bill 95
Cole, George 1
Coleman, Kurt 96
Conley, Bill 85
Conley, Mike, Jr. 66, 93
Conroy, Jim 56
Cooper, John 10, 46, 61,

67, 68
Cordle, Jim 68
Cousineau, Tom 59
Craft, Aaron 31
Croce, Robert 44
Csuri, Charles 86
Curcillo, Tony 60
Dangerfield, Rodney 53
Days, Eddie 16
DeLeone, Jim 81
DeLeone, Tom 91
DeLucia, Brian 3
Dentmon, Justin 94
Dials, Terence 83
Dickerson, Cassie 12
Diebler, Jon 53
Doss, Mike 22, 29
Dudley, Rickey 61
Dye, Tippy 58
Ellison, Leon 94
Ellison, Tiger 50
Fathalikhani, David 57
Fekete, Gene 86
Ferkany, Ed 56
Fesler, Wes 9, 15, 90
Finkes, Matt 13, 67
Foley, Dave 69
Fox, Dustin 2, 29
Fox, Tim 74
Franz, Matt 99
Frey, Greg 10
Fuss-Cheatham, Brandon 83
Galbos, Rich 11
Gamble, Chris 29
Geiger, Andy 67
George, Donna 46
George, Eddie 46, 58, 61, 85
Germaine, Joe 13, 95
Gibbs, Jack 73
Gillespie, Gordie 51
Ginn, Ted, Jr. 5, 92, 96
Glenn, Terry 28, 61
Godfrey, Ernie 35
Gore, Al 95
Gradishar, Randy 6, 56
Graham, Jeff 10
Grange, Red 82
Grant, Cie 2, 64, 78
Greene, Cornelius 6

Griffin, Archie 6, 11, 12, 18, 32, 58, 74, 84, 97, 100
Griffin, James 32
Groom, Andy 78
Groza, Lou 55
Hall, Maurice 5, 52
Hallman, Curley 2
Hanson, Pete 23
Harley, Charles 18
Harris, Walt 13
Hartline, Brian 26
Hartsock, Ben 89
Havlicek, John 36
Hayden, Leophus 37
Hayes, Annie 30, 50
Hayes, Woody 4, 6, 14, 15, 17, 20, 28, 30, 32, 33, 35, 37, 39, 43, 44, 50, 53, 56, 59, 60, 61, 63, 69, 71, 73, 77, 81, 82, 84, 88, 90, 91, 94, 97, 100
Herbstreit, Kirk 75
Hicks, John 100
Hill, Tayler 20, 70
Hines, Jermale 96
Hooley, Bruce 75
Horvath, Les 25, 58, 86
Howe, Gordie 77
Hoying, Bob 61
Hunter, Bob 33
Ingram, Mike 14
Isaman, Derek 99
Jackson, Josh 67
Jackson, Stanley 95
Jacobson, Molly 76
Jacoby, George 30
Jacoby, Nina 30
Janakievski, Vlade 48
Janowicz, Vic 51, 58, 60, 90
Jenkins, Malcolm 26
Jenkins, Michael 38, 89
Jenkins, Pete 57
Johnson, Pete 6
Jones, Jim 91
Joslin, Robert 60
Kalafatis, Linda 27, 45
Karsatos, Jim 40
Katzenmoyer, Andy 67
Kern, Rex

213

17, 33, 37, 50, 69, 88
Killy, Jean-Claude 59
Krenzel, Craig 2, 38, 52, 64, 89
Kriss, Fred 73
Kruezer, Dean 61
Landry, Tom 24
Langhurst, James 47
Larkins, Dick 14
Lassie 15
Lavender, Jantel 70
Leggett, Dave 4, 73
Lemons, Abe 73
Lichter, Eric 54
Lighty, David 66
Lilley, Alexander 1
Lombardi, Vince 52, 74
Long, Billy 69
Lucas, Jerry 36
Mallory, Bill 17
Maravich, Pete 32
Marder, Sam 45
Marti, Yadel 100
Matta, Thad 16, 31, 79, 83, 93
Matte, Tom 39
McCutcheon, Garry 11
McGrath, Dan 8
Menzer, Joe 17, 35, 82
Merchant, Dave 41
Miles, Eddie 10
Miller, Lee 79
Moeller, Tyler 19
Moldea, Emil 9
Moore, Damon 67
Mummey, John 74
Murphy, Austin 52
Murray, Cal 94
Namath, Joe 81
Neal, Chris 76
Nickey, Donnie 29
Nitschke, Ray 42
Nugent, Mike 2
Oden, Greg 66, 93

Ormsby, Maudine 24
Osman, Dan 85
Owens, Jesse 8
Parker, Jim 28
Perdue, Tom 14
Pereson, Ben 68
Petrino, Bobby 7
Pettrey, Aaron 48
Pincura, Stan 21
Prahalis, Samantha 20
Pretorius, Ryan 48
Provost, Ted 69
Pruner, Courtney 27
Pryor, Terrelle 7, 26
Rapp, Jeff 24
Ream, Charlie 47
Reed, William F. 41
Renard, Barney 43
Rico 12
Roach, Woody 74
Robiskie, Brian 54, 58
Rockne, Knute 89
Rogers, Russ 92
Ronemus, Thor 60, 90
Ross, Lydell 2
Ruhl, Bruce 77
Rusnak, Kevin 88
Ryan, Tom 98
Saine, Brandon 54
Sangrey, Shawn 23
Sanzenbacher, Dane 7
Savic, Pandel 9
Schembechler, Bo 6, 39, 71
Schlichter, Art 81
Schmidt, Francis 21, 42
Schumacher, Kurt 63
Scott, Darrion 52
Scott, James 54
Senn, Connor 49
Senn, Lance 49
Skelton, Red 82
Skillings, Vince 94
Skladany, Tom 43

Small, Ray 26, 96
Smith, Katie 70
Smith, Troy 5, 58
Smith, Tucker 21
Smith, Will 52
Snow, Carlos 10
Snook, Jeff 5, 28, 63, 77, 88
Snypp, Wilbur 25, 33
Solomon, Greg 57
Springs, Shawn 61
Springsteen, Bruce 75
Stafford, Mike 3
Stanley, Dimitrious 13, 67
Staysniak, Joe 99
Stillwagon, Jim 17
Stungis, John 80
Sullinger, Jared 53
Swinehart, Rodney 9
Sylvester, Matt 83
Teifke, Howard 65, 80
Terwilliger, Matt 66
Thomas, Solomon 7
Tressel, Jim 5, 26, 34, 38, 52, 58, 62, 64, 68, 72, 78, 86, 96
Truman, Harry 15
Tucker, Ty 62
Turner, Evan 79
Turner, Lana 15
Wagar, Mark 41
Wallace, Rusty 91
Warfield, Paul 14
Watkins, Bobby 4
Waugh, Tom 81
Wells, Beanie 26, 54
Wells, Chris 5
Wells, Jonathan 5
Whisler, Joe 9
White, John 47
White, Stan 37
Widdoes, Carroll 25, 55
Willis, Bill 65
Witte, Luke 41
Wooden, John 50

214